Historic Walk

C000280174

Gibraltar

Second Edition 2013

Edited by Zöe Wildsmith
Cover design by John Wright

ISBN 978-0-9567187-3-0

British Library Cataloguing-in-Publication Data
A catalogue record for this book is available from the British Library.

Published by Destinworld Publishing Ltd.
www.destinworld.com

All photographs in this book are © Angela Doherty unless otherwise stated
angeladoherty1@hotmail.com

Table of contents

Foreword

M y interest in Gibraltar's history began when I was very young, grow-ing up in my childhood home on Crutchett's Ramp, in the heart of the area once known as the Villa Vieja. Before the land border with Spain was fully reopened, there was little else to do than spend my days exploring the centuries-old Moorish Castle and the historic Northern Defences, which were situated right on my doorstep. As I began to venture further afield I soon realized that despite its small size, there was a plethora of interesting historical sites to explore within Gibraltar's 2.5 sq mi and always new places to discover.

Although this book covers all of Gibraltar's main attractions, it hopes to cater for those discerning travellers who are keen to deviate as much as possible from the usual tourist-trail and dig beneath the surface of this fascinating Mediterranean fortress. It operates as a stand-alone travel guide but also aims to inform both first-time visitors and long-time friends of the Rock about Gibraltar's diverse and turbulent history.

The eight themed walks explore every corner of Gibraltar from its guns and defensive fortifications to its Moorish past. They cover the Upper Rock nature reserve, the history of the Royal Navy in Gibraltar and the length of the peninsula from the frontier to Europa Point, as well as a section dealing with nearby Spain. Between them these walks chart a broad spectrum of interests as well as providing a whole host of practical information for visitors to Gibraltar.

Writing this book has been a far more gratifying experience than I could ever have imagined. Not only has it allowed me to rediscover all those corners of Gibraltar that I had not visited since my youth, but it has also taught me a great deal about those places I regularly pass through but have always just taken for granted. I hope therefore that reading this book brings you as much pleasure as writing it has brought me, and that it will help you to fall in love with, or reignite your passion for, Gibraltar: my homeland.

Tristan Cano

– Introduction –
and History

Introduction and History

There can be few destinations throughout the world with a more diverse historical background than Gibraltar's. Visited by millions of tourists each year it is a Mecca for holidaymakers who enjoy the sea and the sunshine while at the same time appealing to those who demand something a little different from their holidays. Getting to grips with the history of Gibraltar's turbulent past provides an excellent backdrop from which to enjoy the many sights and attractions that lend themselves to Gibraltar's present.

The history of human settlement in Gibraltar can be traced back tens of thousands of years to the Stone Age. Gibraltar was thought to have been one of the last sites of regular occupation for Neanderthals and the so-called "Gibraltar Skull", which was blasted out of a quarry on the Rock's north face in 1848, was actually discovered eight years prior to the remains found in Germany's Neander Valley, from where the name Neanderthal comes. A replica of the Gibraltar Skull as well as prehistoric tools and ornaments excavated from the Rock's caves are on display at the Gibraltar Museum. Control of this Mediterranean fortress has passed through many hands, with the Phoenicians, Carthaginians and Romans among those who visited the Rock before its Moorish conquest in AD 711. The initial incursion into Europe was led by a Berber general named Tariq ibn-Ziyad and there have been theories that suggest that it was after him (Jabal Tariq meaning literally Mountain of Tariq) that the rock known by the Romans as Mons Calpe took its eventual name of Gibraltar.

The Moors enjoyed Gibraltar's strategic importance for around three quarters of a millennium and there is still plenty of evidence of their time on the Rock. The most prominent remnant is the Moorish Castle whose Tower of Homage overlooks the isthmus on the north-west side of the Rock and is undoubtedly one of Gibraltar's most well-known landmarks. The precise origins of the Castle are not known, but work on the original structure was said to have been completed by Tariq himself in 742, which would make it the first Moorish fortification ever constructed on European soil. Work on the present structure is not thought to have begun until the 11th century, with much having been constructed centuries later, around the early 14th century.

The Moors' 700-year occupation of the Rock ended when Gibraltar was ceded to Castilian forces in 1462. Much of the original Moorish architecture was destroyed and built upon during the subsequent years of Spanish rule, and the British continued this from 1704 onwards. An example of this is the

Roman Catholic Cathedral of St Mary the Crowned, built by order of Queen Isabella on the site of Gibraltar's main Mosque. The Cathedral, having been rebuilt or extensively altered on a number of occasions presents a curious blend of British and Spanish architecture, however the small courtyard is the one remaining vestige of the Mosque's original court.

The most notable Spanish addition is Charles V Wall, which stands at the southern end of Main Street adjacent to the Trafalgar Cemetery. The wall, which dates back to 1550 and was originally built to keep out Barbary pirates, was recently refurbished and offers an alternative walking route from the area known as the Apes Den to the summit of the Rock. Many of Gibraltar's defences were destroyed during attacks on the Rock following its capture by an Anglo-Dutch force in 1704. During the Great Siege of Gibraltar (1779–1783), the British Garrison survived an almost complete blockade of supplies and numerous assaults destroying much of the city, including the Cathedral. The Great Siege Tunnels, which were instrumental in the British defence of the Rock are now a fully-accessible tourist attraction and are complemented in the Upper Rock by a City Under Siege exhibition, which gives a fascinating insight into life in Gibraltar during the early years of British occupation.

In 1805, following the Battle of Trafalgar, HMS Victory was towed to Gibraltar with the body of Admiral Nelson onboard, famously preserved in a casket of rum. The series of batteries known as Parson's Lodge, which stand on a limestone shelf above Rosia Bay, are often overlooked by visitors to the Rock but are a must-see attraction, particularly for military enthusiasts seeking a unique view of what was Nelson's anchorage. Visitors should also be sure to visit the so-called "100-ton gun", a monster piece of military machinery that lies derelict on the nearby Napier of Magdala Battery. The Trafalgar Cemetery adjacent to Charles V Wall by Southport Gate contains the remains of military personnel who died in Trafalgar and other nearby naval battles. The cemetery itself is a peaceful spot that provides a refreshing sanctuary from the commotions of Gibraltar's busy city centre.

The Upper Rock is undoubtedly the best place to explore the many abandoned buildings and gun installations that represent Gibraltar's more recent military history. Few are better preserved than the 9.2-inch, Mark X guns, which can be seen at O'Hara's Battery and which, at an altitude of 426m, are the highest gun emplacement on the Rock. Having been restored, much of the gun's original mechanisms remain intact and this fascinating example of early 20th century artillery coupled with the spectacular 360-degree views from the Battery make it a must-see for anyone visiting the Rock. There are plenty more examples of 20th century military installations on the Upper

Rock including the impressive World War II guns at Princess Anne's Battery and the derelict remains of some smaller weapons that can be viewed on Royal Anglian Way.

Throughout the centuries, many thousands of lives were lost in defence of the Rock, with thousands more perishing in often disastrous attempts to conquer this most coveted of prizes. But Gibraltar is so much more than just the gatekeeper to the Mediterranean or the sum total of the walls and bastions that make up this fortress town. The iconic Rock itself has been marvelled upon by travellers for many millennia and remains the centrepiece of Gibraltar's tourist product. This lump of Jurassic limestone in the south of Europe and just 22km from the North African mainland is itself a cradle of ancient civilizations; a cradle of history.

Getting There

Gibraltar is visited by over 8 million people each year, ranging from day-trippers to those who visit the Rock for a week or more at a time.

A valid EU passport is required to gain entry into Gibraltar although entry is also possible without a visa from countries such as the USA, Australia and Canada. As a general rule however, individuals from countries who require a visa for entry to the UK will also require a separate visa in order to enter Gibraltar. If in doubt, you can always check Gibraltar's visa requirements by contacting Gibraltar's Immigration Section before travelling.

Applications for visas should be made at the British Embassy located in the applicant's country of residence or via the visa section of the UK Passport Office in London. Applications should be accompanied by a valid passport with at least 2 blank pages, proof of a hotel reservation and a copy of the return ticket together with a fee.

Immigration Section (Gibraltar)
Joshua Hassan House
Secretary's Lane, Gibraltar
Tel. +350 200 51725 and +350 200 76948
Fax +350 200 43053
E-mail *immigration.csro@gibraltar.gov.gi*

The London Passport Office
Globe House
89 Eccleston Square
London
SW1V 1PN
Tel. +44 300 222 0000 (from within the UK)

By Air

Gibraltar is served by its own airport. British Airways flies daily to Gibraltar from London Heathrow (see *www.ba.com* for further details). In addition low-cost carriers Monarch Airlines (*www.flymonarch.com*) and Easy-jet (*www.easyjet.com*) fly regularly from London Luton and London Gatwick airports respectively. Monarch Airlines also have a three-times weekly service from Manchester. In addition Monarch Airlines will be commencing a three times weekly service to East Midlands Airport.

The Spanish airports in Malaga and Jerez are both just over an hour's drive from Gibraltar. Both airports offer flights to a far wider list of countries including many European and North American destinations. For details on these airports, including the destinations and airlines they serve, see the website of Aena, the Spanish state-owned company that owns and manages all Spanish airports (*www.aena.es*).

Unlike the busy airport in Malaga, Gibraltar's new state of the art Air Terminal (inaugurated in May 2011) is compact and it is very easy to find one's way around. There will usually be taxis waiting just outside the terminal building but there is also the option of taking a bus from the opposite side of the road or simply walking into the town area.

By Road

 The rugged tip of the Rock of Gibraltar is difficult to miss as you make your way south along the Costa del Sol or Spain's south-western coastline.

When travelling towards Gibraltar on the A7 or the AP-7 toll from Malaga, continue as the road becomes the E-15 and follow signs for Alcaidesa/La Línea. When you come off the slip road, turn left and pass under the motorway before following signs for Gibraltar. It is hard to overlook the rock of Gibraltar that dramatically juts out of the landscape and is illuminated by large spotlights in the evenings.

Should you miss this exit, you can always take the following exit (San Roque/La Línea). At the end of the slip road, turn right and follow the service road that continues alongside the motorway. When you get to the end of the service road, turn onto the motorway and take the far left lane in order to take a sharp left turn within about 50 metres of getting onto the road. This route is therefore best avoided as this manoeuvre can be tricky at times, particularly during busy periods. Once you have done this, bear right onto the CA-34 and follow the road to Gibraltar that passes through Campamento and along La Línea's western coast on the Avenida de España.

The Border Queue

The frontier that separates Gibraltar from Spain can get extremely busy, especially during peak times or in the summer months when thousands of tourists visit the Rock. It is impossible to say with any certainty at what times of the day the vehicle queue will be shortest, but the longest queues entering Gibraltar tend to be during the weekends or on weekday mornings as commuters and day trippers make their way in. The worst queues leaving Gibraltar are between the hours of 16:00 and 20:00 on week days. Be prepared for an approximate half-hour wait if crossing in or out of Gibraltar in a vehicle during any of these peak times.

The queue curls around a loop on the Western coast at the end of Avenida de España and sometimes continues up the Avenida to the Palacio de Congresos, which is the large building you can see next to the Asur (formerly Iberostar) Hotel. So if you see a large queue of cars as you begin to make your approach to Gibraltar, the chances are that this is the back end of the queue. Queue-jumping is thoroughly frowned upon.

A reasonable alternative may be to leave your car in one of the many inexpensive paid-for parkings in La Línea and walk across the border on foot. This way you can avoid the queues altogether and a direct bus (£1.00 single, or £1.50 for all day travel) or taxi (approximately £5.00) can take you to the city centre in about five minutes or you can walk it in about twenty.

Note also that entry to Gibraltar is free of charge so do not be duped into purchasing an entry from any of the unscrupulous "entrepreneurs" who work the Spanish side of the border.

By Bus

The Spanish Bus company Automoviles Portillo operates from the bus station in La Línea de la Concepción, just a five-minute walk from the border with Gibraltar. A direct bus service operates to the Andalusian cities of Malaga, Seville, Granada and Cadiz with connections from these cities onto the whole of Spain. A direct local bus service also exists between La Línea and the nearby towns of San Roque, and Guadiaro as well as the cities of Algeciras and Tarifa for ferries to Morocco. For a more detailed overview of the bus service within Gibraltar, see Getting Around.

By Train

While Gibraltar is not connected to a rail network, the RENFE rail network in Spain offers an efficient rail route between Spain's major cities. The closest Spanish rail station to Gibraltar is in Estación de San Roque, which is on the scenic RENFE line from Algeciras to Bobadilla junction, via Ronda. The train station is Estacion de San Roque is about a 15 minute drive from the border.

Travellers can take the train from London to nearby Algeciras by contacting Rail Europe Travel Centre in the UK.

Rail Europe Travel Centre
178 Piccadilly
London W1J 9AL
www.raileurope.co.uk
Tel. +44 870 5848 848
E-mail *reservations@raileurope.co.uk*

Train tickets for the RENFE network in Spain can be purchased from Spanish Railways UK, the official RENFE sales agents in the UK:

Spanish Railways UK
Regent House Business Centre
24-25 Nutford Place
Marble Arch
London W1H 5YN
www.spanish-rail.co.uk
Tel. +44 20 7224 0345
E-mail *enquiries@spanish-rail.co.uk*
For train timetables and fares in English: *www.renfe.es/ingles*

 By Boat

Gibraltar is a very popular cruise ship destination with cruise liners stopping over to visit the Rock on almost every day of the year.

However despite being almost completely surrounded by water, Gibraltar is not served by regular passenger routes to Africa or any other European destinations. In fact there is only one "regular" ferry service from Gibraltar to Tangiers (contact Tourafrica on tel. +350 200 77666) and this service can be termed inefficient, even at the best of times. A much better way to get to Morocco is via the nearby ports of Algeciras or Tarifa situated across the Bay and about 20 and 40 minutes' drive from Gibraltar respectively. Several ferry companies operate out of these ports (Balearia – *www.balearia.com* – and Trasmediterranea – *www.trasmediterranea.es* – provide two of the most popular services) transporting over 3.5 million passengers across the Straits between them.

Ferries depart several times a day and normally take about 2 hours, with faster ferry services taking closer to 45 minutes. There are also regular daily routes to the Spanish enclave of Ceuta on the African mainland. If you are arriving on board your own vessel, there are two main marinas in Gibraltar. The first is Ocean Village/Marina Bay (VHF Channel 73), which offer reasonably priced day rates which vary by season and which can accomodate vessels of most lengths including the largest super yachts. Ocean Village has around 200 berths, each with a facility point with fresh water, electricity and a telephone line. Shower and toilet facilities are also available nearby at the pier office building and wireless internet access is also available via prepaid cards. The Marina complex offers a fine selection of restaurants and bars onshore as well as other services such as shops, a laundrette and a medical clinic. Gibraltar's casino is also located in close proximity.

Queensway Quay (also on VHF Channel 73) is a smaller marina with 185 fully serviced berths which can accommodate up to eight 30 metre and two 40 metre boats. Set against the backdrop of luxury residential developments, this marina offers a choice of trendy restaurants and bars along the Queensway Quay waterfront. The marina also boasts a chandlery, a marine electronics company, a sailing school and a laundrette. It can only accommodate yachts up to 80m in length and has a minimum depth of 3.5m.

Diesel is available at very competitive prices from the Shell and BP stations at Waterport Wharf, which can be found on your right as you approach Ocean Village/Marina Bay. Next to the Shell refuelling station are the Immigration Office and Customs Reception Berth, to which all yachts berthing at Ocean Village/Marina Bay should report. Boats berthing at Queensway Quay should report to Customs in the Marina's office. Yacht repair facilities on the Rock are provided by M. Sheppard & Co Ltd.

Marinas

....

Ocean Village/Marina Bay
Marina Bay
Gibraltar
Tel. +350 200 73300
www.marinabay.gi

Queensway Quay Marina
Queensway
Gibraltar
Tel. +350 200 78780
www.queenswayquay.com

Other Useful Contacts

....

Port Captain
Port Office
North Mole
Gibraltar
Tel. +350 200 77254

Port Operations Room and Enquiries
Tel. +350 200 78134 or +350 200 77004

M. Sheppard & Co. Ltd
Yacht Repairs
Coaling Island
Gibraltar
Tel. +350 200 76895
www.sheppard.gi

Getting Around

Practically every corner of Gibraltar is accessible on foot. The city centre is compact and even the Upper Rock and the beaches on the eastern side of the Rock can be easily reached without needing to rely on transport. In any event, the narrow streets in Gibraltar's Upper Town area are not the best place to drive and finding that elusive car parking space is a tough proposition at the best of times. Be warned however that during the warm summer months walking around is not as easy as it is during cooler weather. For information on getting around by taxi, please refer to the chapter on Tours.

Gibraltar by Bus

Blue Bus Service
Gibraltar's old-fashioned bus system became a thing of the past in April 2004, replaced by a fleet of modern air-conditioned, blue-liveried buses. This bus system is fairly efficient and easy to use while offering access to practically every corner of Gibraltar. The Blue bus service in Gibraltar is cheap and easy to use, accommodating disabled passengers, prams and shoppers carrying heavy loads.

Gibraltar Bus Company
Bus Depot
Winston Churchill Avenue
P.O. Box 3000
Gibraltar
Tel. +350 200 47622
Fax +350 200 47626
E-mail *info@gibraltarbuscompany.gi*

Red Bus Service
In addition to the blue buses that service the whole of the Rock, there are also the red double-decker Route 10 buses operated by Calypso Travel. The Route 10 buses run from the frontier to the Morrisons Superstore at Europort and also stop near the Old Naval Ground by the City War Memorial.
Monday: Departs Frontier 8.15am-8pm (approx. every 15 minutes)
Friday: Departs British War Memorial (Reclamation Road) 8.30am-8pm
(approx. every 15 minutes)

Saturday: Departs Frontier 8.40am-7.20pm (approx. every 30 minutes) and British War Memorial 9.10am-7.10pm (approx. every 30 minutes)
Sunday: 9.45am-6pm shuttle service

Calypso Travel
Suite 5
1st Floor Leon House
Secretary's Lane
Gibraltar
Tel. +350 200 76520
Fax +350 200 77362

Gibraltar by Car

Driving in Gibraltar can be a nightmare for anyone who comes unprepared. Narrow roads, one-way systems and badly parked cars conspire to trouble even the most experienced of motorists. In addition rush-hour traffic, particularly in the afternoon between 4.30-8pm and in the vicinity of the airport can be a nightmare to negotiate. For these reasons visitors who travel in from Spain are often advised to park their cars in La Línea and walk across the border, enjoying Gibraltar's sights either by bus, taxi or of course, on foot.

Some may argue that nothing beats having access to your own car and this option certainly gives visitors some flexibility during their visit to the Rock. Motorists driving into Gibraltar must have a valid driving licence, vehicle insurance and the vehicle's certificate of registration (log-book). It should be noted that the Royal Gibraltar Police can be extremely vigilant when it comes to road safety and as such the highway code should be observed and respected at all times. Driving in Gibraltar is on the right hand side of the road and there is a maximum speed limit of 50km/h (30mph), except within the city walls and in most residential estates where the speed limit is 30km/h (18mph). There are regular police speed checks and the police will soon be able to give on-the-spot fines to motorists. Furthermore, seat belts, if installed in the vehicle, should be worn in the front and rear at all times.

Parking can be a particular problem for motorists and successive governments have unsuccessfully attempted to control the problems caused by the increasing numbers of vehicles on Gibraltar's roads. There is plenty of roadside parking but spaces are hard to find, so if you are looking for a free parking spot you are best off searching for one of the free-to-use car parks.

There is one at the Grand Paradeand one on Queensway as well as near the beaches on the Eastern side of the Rock. Parking restrictions are strictly enforced by the police, traffic wardens and private security companies. A parking ticket given by a traffic warden or police officer will usually set you back £15 however a ticket in one of the new 'blue' zones or on private property could land you a clamp or a fine of up to £50. If your car is towed away, contact Gibraltar Security Services Ltd on the number listed below.

Paid-for parking is relatively inexpensive and car parks on Bayside Road and at the International Commercial Centre (ICC) will usually allow a few hours parking for about £3 or £4.

There are various petrol stations, though these tend to be concentrated on the northern end of Gibraltar on Winston Churchill Avenue or near the runway. Morrisons supermarket has a petrol station and there is also a small BP garage in the South District near the South Jumpers Bastion at the base of Scud Hill.

Gibraltar Security Services Limited
Queensway Car Park
Reclamation Road
Gibraltar
Tel. +350 200 76999
Out of hours +350 588 57000

Gibraltar by Bike

With its steep inclines, heavy road traffic and complete lack of bicycle lanes, Gibraltar is not what you would consider the perfect destination for cycling. Whilst more accomplished cyclists may enjoy the route to the top of the Rock, its certainly not a route for the amateur cyclist who may find themselves frustrated by the limitations of Gibraltar City Centre cycling. Notwithstanding the above, cycling is increasing in popularity amongst more eco-friendly sections of the locals popularity and the 'GibiBikes' scheme launched in 2012, similar to the so-called 'Boris-Bikes' in London, offer members the opportunity to make use of a bank of public bicycles located at 19 key locations around the Rock. At present, the scheme is intended to be available to locals only, however membership can be applied for by anyone with an address in Gibraltar. Whilst use of this service may not be feasible for short-term visitors to the Rock, those who are staying for a longer period may find GibiBikes to be a good way to get around during their stay. Prospective members of the scheme should apply via the GibiBikes website which contains the terms and conditions of service as well as the GibiBikes code of conduct and a map of bike station locations.

GibiBikes

List of locations include: The Frontier, Victoria Stadium, Waterport Road, Eurotowers, Reclamation Road, Commonwealth Parade car park, Rosia Road, Grand Parade car park, Southport Gates, Line Wall Road, Market Place, Eastern Beach Road, Catalan Bay, St. Josephs School, Europa Point and Rosia Parade.

Tel. +350 200 60222 (8.30am to 5.30pm)
Email. info@gibibikes.gi
www.gibibikes.gi

– Walk I –
Pre-20th-Century
British Military History

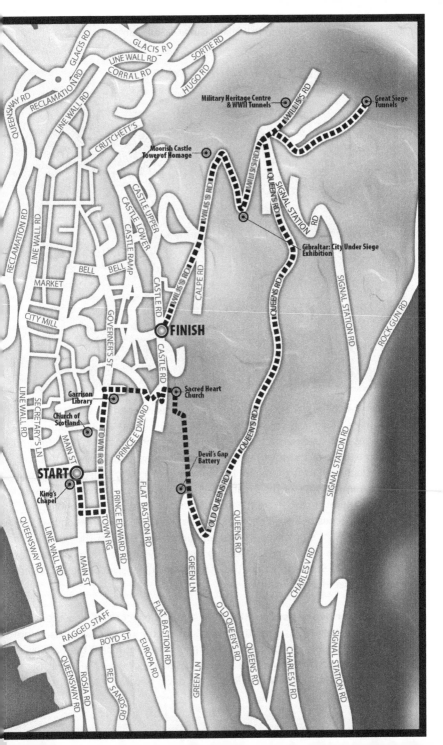

Gibraltar had been under Spanish rule for 242 years when, in 1704, an Anglo-Dutch force under the command of Admiral Sir George Rooke captured the poorly-guarded garrison from Spain. Nine years later, in 1713, "the full and entire propriety of the town and castle of Gibraltar, together with the port, fortifications, and forts thereunto belonging" was formally ceded to the Crown of Britain in Article X of the Treaty of Utrecht. When the British first arrived very few improvements were made to Gibraltar's existing fortifications, however as the needs of the garrison and the growing civilian population began to change, the Rock's defences were slowly improved. Many of the buildings in Gibraltar's town area were built during the early years of British rule and as the threat from Spain increased, the armoury and defensive fortifications were also developed during this time.

Getting your bearings: This walk begins at the Convent at the southern end of Main Street and runs from the lower town to the upper town area before following the pedestrian footpath to the Upper Rock. From here the walk takes in several attractions within the Nature Reserve including the Great Siege Tunnels before following Willis's Road back down to town.

Length: Approximately 3km/1.8mi (2.5 hours)

*Stand outside the Angry Friar pub and face down Main Street (in a northern direction) and you will see on your left hand side the Governor of Gibraltar's official residence on the Rock, known locally as **the Convent**.*

This building took its name from a Convent of Franciscan Friars that was built on this site in 1480 and remained here until Gibraltar was taken by the British. According to local legend the Convent is haunted by a spiritual presence; the so-called "Grey Lady", a Franciscan nun who was caught trying to elope with her sweetheart. The Convent itself is not open to visitors except on special open days held approximately once a year. **King's Chapel** however, to the right of the Convent's main entrance is open to the public. When the Convent became the Governor's official residence in 1728, the chapel was also taken over and became the first place of Anglican worship in Gibraltar.

The Chapel is a charming little space adorned with many artefacts of historical significance. For example the crests and badges at the entrance to the Chapel represent the many corps that have served on the Rock and the sanctuary colours on the eastern wall enshrine the names of all the regiments who have distinguished themselves in battle down the years, either during the taking of Gibraltar or in its protection. Visitors will note also the

Queen Anne Communion Set displayed in a glass-fronted alcove in the Chapel's sanctuary. It bears the Royal Arms of Queen Anne and a 1710 hallmark, making it probably the first communion set to be given to the Chapel after the capture of Gibraltar.

Kings Chapel

Main Street, Gibraltar
Telephone: +350 200 53592
Open to the public: Monday-Saturday, 9.30am-5.30pm
Mass is held on Saturday at 5.45pm (Roman Catholic Mass) and Sunday at 10.30am (Anglican Mass).

The Convent is guarded by a sentry from the Royal Gibraltar Regiment from Monday to Thursday, 9am-4pm and on Fridays from 9am-1pm with intermittent Changing of the Guard ceremonies held outside the **Convent Guard Room** opposite the Convent itself. There is also a ceremonial Changing of the Guard held about three times a year with the Royal Gibraltar Regiment Band and His Excellency the Governor in attendance. Further information on times and dates for these can be obtained from the Gibraltar Tourist Information Centre at Casemates Square. You will note outside the guard room two brass cannons dating from 1840, which are splendidly maintained by the Royal Gibraltar Regiment.

From Kings Chapel, continue south on Main Street in the direction of Charles V Wall.

You will see on the left hand side of the street a curious little shop called **Benzaquen Antiques** (295 Main Street, open Monday–Friday, 9am-7pm). A visit to this tiny, grotto-like bazaar is a walk through local history, with its many interesting Gibraltar-themed prints, miniature cannons and other old military paraphernalia.

A few metres on from the antique shop, turn east (in the direction of the Rock) and make your way up Victualling Office Lane onto Town Range, a street that was once one of Gibraltar's most important thoroughfares and contains many fine examples of British colonial architecture.

The buildings on either side of the summit of Victualling Office Lane were the old army victualling office and the army bakery.

Turn left and you will notice a series of buildings on your right hand side that collectively make up the Town Range Barracks and were originally built in 1740 to provide accommodation for soldiers and elegant pavilions for their commanding officers.

You will note Officers Quarters No II followed by a building that is now St Mary's Infant School. Town Range is still known locally as Calle Cuartel, which literally means "Barracks Street". On your left, opposite the School is the rear of **No. 6 Convent Place**, the office of Gibraltar's Chief Minister and therefore perhaps Gibraltar's equivalent to London's Whitehall.

Continue north on Town Range you will see Officers Quarters No III and a continuation of the barracks.

This particular stretch of the building had fallen into general disrepair before being tastefully renovated and transformed into stylish city centre residential and commercial accommodation. The symmetry of the barracks is tainted somewhat by a mid-Victorian building that was erected between the third and fourth Officers' Quarters and is now occupied by a local barrister's chambers.

*Continue north on Town Range (keeping the Rock on your right hand side) you will reach **St Andrew's Church**, part of the Presbytery of Europe under the Church of Scotland.*

This lovely little church was built, largely of limestone, in the mid-19th century, when there was a substantial number of Scottish regiments on the Rock. While numerous alterations have been made to the Church throughout the years it still boasts the original pulpit, pews and baptismal font from the 1854 construction.

On the northern interior wall of the Church can be found the regimental plaques of various battalions that have served on the Rock and who maintain special connections with the Church. Also of note are the three beautiful stained glass windows that were installed in 1953 and can be seen from the exterior of the building on Town Range.

St Andrew's Church of Scotland

Governors Parade
Gibraltar
Tel. +350 200 77040
Open: Daily, 11am-1pm
Mass held: Sunday at 10.30am

The area directly in front of the Church is known as **Governor's Parade** and was originally part of the Governor's garden where his horses and cattle would be left to graze. It has also been known as Gunner's Parade and the French Parade in reference to the stunning garden that stood on the site of the present theatre and was landscaped by a French gardener. The area has been heavily developed in recent years and is now mainly used as a car park as well as being the drive-way to the O'Callaghan Eliott Hotel.

Have a look at the memorial to Queen Victoria in the Eliott Hotel's veranda area. This was designed by an Italian sculptor called Lazzarini and erected in 1910. The tiled square at the far end of Governor's Parade is known locally as *la Piazella* and was the site of the once spectacular **Theatre Royal**. The theatre opened in 1847 with a performance of Verdi's *Nabucodonosor* and went on to host many well-known operas and performers including a visit in 1946 from Italian tenor Beniamino Gigli, widely regarded as one of the best opera tenors of all time. The Theatre Royal fell into disrepair and a recent major refurbishment was anticipated, maintaining the theatre's

original façade. Sadly, the project was abandoned before completion and now the front of the building is all that remains of what was once the centre of cultural life in Gibraltar.

Remaining on Governor's Parade, while standing at the summit of Library Street (which leads from Main Street), you will be able to see the former **offices of the Gibraltar Chronicle**, which still bear the newspaper's name. The *Gibraltar Chronicle*'s first bulletin was released on May 4, 1801 under the heading "*Continuation of the Intelligence from Egypt*" and included a list of the casualties from the British army's Egyptian Campaign. The *Chronicle* is the world's second oldest English language newspaper to have been in continuous print, beaten only by *The Times* (of London). On October 24, 1805 the *Gibraltar Chronicle* released its greatest scoop when a special edition printed in both French and English announced the news of the British victory at the Battle of Trafalgar and the death of Admiral Nelson.

Adjacent to the former *Gibraltar Chronicle* offices is the **Garrison Library**, which was originally founded in 1793 and housed in premises on Main Street before being relocated to its present purpose-built location in 1804. The library was the brainchild of Captain John Drinkwater who was the author of probably one of the most well-known histories of the Great Siege of Gibraltar. Since there were no bookshops in Gibraltar at that time, Drinkwater saw the need for

a good circulating library to save officers stationed on the Rock from "*having their minds enervated and vitiated by dissipation*". The library was originally formed with books donated by stationed officers, as well as cash donations from then Governor General Sir Robert Boyd and Lieutenant Governor Major-General O'Hara who was to go on to become "the most munificent Patron of the Institution".

The impressive stone-built colonial-style building is set in a small yet pleasant garden, which offers a relaxing sanctuary from the hustle and bustle of the surrounding city centre. The building itself is two stories high and is perhaps best appreciated by taking a guided tour. Much of the building's interior layout remains unchanged since the 19th century as can be seen from the lithograph of the Large Room, which shows the brass telescope, the portrait of Colonel Drinkwater and many articles of furniture in their current positions. Another notable relic of bygone days is the sandglass that appears in the lithograph and is now kept in the Secretary's Office. This piece of equipment was used to determine the not-insignificant matter of how long each member would be allocated the Library's copy of *The Times* newspaper. Nowadays, the Library is a fully-functioning research library and parts of it can be hired out to host small functions.

The Garrison Library

....

Governor's Parade
Gibraltar
Tel. +350 200 77418
Open: Monday-Thursday, 9am-5pm, Friday, 9am-3pm. Guided Tours
on Fridays at 11am; personal tours can be arranged at other times.
Entry and tours are free of charge although a donation is welcomed.

*From the Garrison Library you should follow **Library Ramp**, which is the*
steep slope adjacent to the building.

This ramp is still known colloquially as Balali, which is a corruption of "Ball Alley" referring to the Garrison Racquet Court and Billiards Club that existed up until 1869 in roughly the area where no. 8, Library Ramp now stands. Before starting your ascent, it is worth noting the building that stands opposite the Library that now houses, among other things, a kitchen showroom. The building was built in 1825 by the executors of the late John Gavino's estate as can be seen from an interesting shield that hangs above the entrance to the building opposite the London Bar.

The structures that previously stood on this spot, known as Boyd's buildings, had the rather dubious honour of being the source of the spread of Gibraltar's 1804 yellow fever epidemic. The story goes that a shopkeeper by the name of Santos who was a resident of the building picked up the virus on a business trip to Cadiz. Within a week, as a result of the bad hygiene levels endured by the lower class residents of the tenement, the disease spread, eventually causing the deaths of 860 military personnel on the Rock and almost 5,000 civilians, a sizeable chunk of Gibraltar's total population at the time.

Library Ramp is home to several interesting colonial properties including a residence known as **Library House** and that known as **Mediterranean Terrace**, which from 1897-1925 was the Garrison's private member's club, known as the Mediterranean Club.

When you reach the top of the ramp, turn right onto Prince Edward's Road,
a road that took its name from the fourth son of King George III who served
in Gibraltar as colonel of the Royal Fusiliers. At the crossroads you will see
a small shop called Carters at the junction and it may be worth picking up
some refreshments from here as opportunities to do so become scarcer as

you continue further along this walk. Turn Left onto Lime Kiln Road and you will soon notice the imposing **Sacred Heart Church** on your right hand side opposite the old Police Barracks, which are an early 20th-century construction and unfortunately lie derelict. Follow the steps that lead up to the Church and walk alongside its western wall towards its main entrance.

The Church is aligned to the Roman Catholic faith and was built in the Gothic style in 1874, in the style of Notre Dame Cathedral in Paris. The Church was built using stone imported from Malta, which was at the time still a British colony. A walk around the interior is recommended, with its beautiful 19th-century Italian marble altar being a particular point of note, together with a charming statue of the Virgin Mary by the main entrance.

Sacred Heart Parish Church

3 Lime Kiln Road
Gibraltar
Tel. +350 200 73709
Mass held: Monday to Friday at 7pm in Spanish
Saturday at 7pm in English
Sunday at 11am (English) and 7pm (Spanish)

Near its main entrance, there is a small path that leads away from the Church onto Devils Gap Road, a colourful set of large steps known locally as "**Union Jack Steps**". These steps were painted in red, white and blue to mark the occasion of Gibraltar's first referendum, which was held on September 10,

1967. Gibraltarians were asked whether they wished to pass under Spanish sovereignty or remain British and voted overwhelmingly in favour of the latter with only 44 voters choosing to align with Spain. Gibraltar still celebrates September 10 each year as its National Day, a public holiday in Gibraltar since 1992. A second referendum was held in 2002 with a similarly resounding 99% of Gibraltarians rejecting the proposal of shared sovereignty with Spain.

The Steps turn into a rough track that is the quickest route on foot into the **Upper Rock Nature Reserve**, *which can be reached after a fifteen minute hike followed by a sharp left turn onto Old Queen's Road at the end of the rough path.*

The first sight you will see in the Upper Rock is **Devils Gap Battery**, which stands at a height of 131 m above sea level and provides excellent views of the Bay of Gibraltar as well as the town area below, including the naval dockyard to the south. The battery is built on the site of a former Spanish platform that was known as Punta del Diablo or "Devil's Point". There you will find two 6-inch BL Mk VII coastal defence guns, which remain in relatively good condition considering that they have been decommissioned for over 50 years. To the rear of the southern gun is an underground complex of buildings, which retain many

original features however, due to the poor state of the buildings you should proceed with caution if you choose to explore this area (for more information on Devil's Gap Battery see Walk 5: The Guns of Gibraltar).

After leaving Devils Gap Battery continue to ascend Old Queens Road until you reach another junction on which you can see a short flight of steps leading to the entrance of Ince's Farm.

This property on the Upper Rock is now privately owned and is therefore inaccessible to the public. Nevertheless it is worthy of mention as it was this plot of land that was awarded in 1783 to Sergeant Major Ince, the architect of the Great Siege Tunnels in recognition of his contribution to the defence of Gibraltar.

*The steeper of the two roads, heading south (to the right) leads to the area known as the **Ape's Den**, which is worthy of a short diversion. Before turning left and proceeding in a northerly direction, you may wish to follow the adjacent path that leads to an abandoned battery and gun emplacement and offers interesting views of the south-west of the city. This is a perfect picnic spot when not populated by the cheeky Barbary macaques.*

From Ince's Farm, turn left and follow Queens Road past various look-outs and picnic areas before reaching **Princess Caroline's Battery***, a battery built in 1732 and named after King George II's third daughter.*

The Battery was adapted to its current form in the early 1900s to accommodate guns similar to the ones at Devil's Gap Battery and which have since been removed. You will note the upper projection of is built on the site of the former Willis's Guard Room and a plaque marks the spot where this once stood. The interior of Princess Caroline's Battery now also houses the **Military Heritage Centre**, a small exhibition with some interesting displays including weaponry and other relics of the Great Siege. The back chamber, known as the Memorial Chamber, is a touching tribute to all those who have served in the armed forces through the years in the protection of the Rock.

Princess Caroline's Battery is also where one of two **World War II Tunnel** tours begins. During World War II British Gibraltar was thought to be an obvious target for attack by Germany and its allies. Much of the civilian population of Gibraltar was evacuated and Gibraltar once again took up a key role in naval operations in the Mediterranean. Prior to the outbreak of World War II, the Royal Engineers had been excavating a network of tunnels within the Rock itself, building as it were, a city within a city. There are approximately 32 miles of tunnels running through the Rock and the World War II Tunnels guided tour allows you to travel into the very bowels of the Rock, not only to marvel at the feat of modern engineering the tunnels are, but also to show what life would have been like within the tunnels during wartime. A more extensive tunnels tour can be arranged with a specialist guide by ringing the Gibraltar Tourist Office (see Tours section).

Rock and Fortress Tunnel Tour

Hay's Level
Gibraltar
Tel. +350 200 45957
Open: Monday–Saturday, 10.30am-5.30pm
Prices: £8 for an hour long guided tour

From Princess Caroline's Battery you can follow the road up to the Siege Tunnels or, down towards **Princess Anne's Battery***, which is probably the most extensive gun battery on the northern side of the Rock.*

Princess Anne's Battery con-sists of four 5.25-inch AA guns and is the only intact battery of this type anywhere in the world. Unfortunately due to persistent vandalism of the site, Princess Anne's Battery has not been opened to the public since its most re-cent renovation several years ago. Access to the Battery

therefore needs to be arranged through the Gibraltar tourist office and the doors to the machine rooms and magazines have now been welded shut. You will also note adjacent to the steel doors that give access to the Battery, another restricted area con-taining a large building complex with numerous curved roofs. This partially subterranean magazine, which is said to be the largest of its type remaining anywhere in the world, has unfortunately fallen into disrepair and is also inaccessible to visitors.

*Turn left and follow the steep incline until you reach the **Great Siege Tunnels**, also known as the Upper Galleries.*

This network of tunnels, built by the Company of Soldier Artificers who were the precursors of the Royal Engineers, was excavated during the Great Siege, which lasted from 1779 to 1783. The governor of Gibraltar, General Eliott, was said to have offered a reward to anyone who could figure out a method for getting guns onto a notch on the northern face of the Rock. An ambi-tious young sergeant major by the name of Henry Ince suggested that this could be achieved by tunnelling along the contour of the Rock. This idea was adapted further almost inadvertently when vents were blasted to let air into the tunnel, creating further embrasures on which to place guns. As a result of his ingenuity Ince was given a commission and a plot of land that still bears his name, as well as the gift of a "valuable horse" by the Duke of Kent (Queen Victoria's father).

You will see an impressive Victorian 64-pounder gun on its original car-riage by the entrance to the Upper Galleries, dating back to 1850. There are various other guns of the same age within the Galleries, as well as an older 18th-century cannon.

About 200m into the tunnel is a large chamber known as St George's Hall,

which contained several gun embrasures. This is the interior of the so-called "notch" and it was here that Lord Napier of Magdala held a banquet in honour of visiting US president, General Ulysses S. Grant.

The so-called Holyland Tunnel (which posts east in the direction of Mecca, the Holy Land) would usually have led from St. George's Hall to an observation platform above the fishing village of Catalan Bay on the east side of the Rock, however this part of the Great Siege Tunnels is currently closed for renovation.

Great Siege Tunnels

Upper Rock Nature Reserve
Gibraltar
Open: Daily, 9.30am-7pm
Prices: Entry to the Upper Rock Nature Reserve costs £10 (adults) and £5 (children) and includes St Michael's Cave, City Under Siege Exhibition, the Moorish Castle and the Great Siege Tunnels.

Exiting the Great Siege Tunnels, start your descent back to Princess Caroline's Battery and then continue down on Willis's Road, which leads from the Upper Rock to the Upper Town area. About 50m down Willis's Road, before the hill makes a sharp right turn, you will see a well-preserved 19th-

century **Lime Kiln** *on your left hand side.*

Kilns of this nature were very common in Gibraltar in the 1900s and this is the only remaining example of those that existed dotted around the Rock at this time. They were used to produce lime that was either used to whitewash buildings or was poured over dead bodies to prevent the spread of disease.

A further 10m down the road is the **Gibraltar - A City Under Siege** *exhibition, housed in* **Willis's Magazine**.

The magazine was constructed during the early part of the 18th century to manufacture and store ammunition and is believed to be one of the earliest buildings to have been built during the British occupation of the Rock. One of the most notable features of the building is its drainage system, which has been well restored offering visitors an accurate display of how such systems would have operated nearly 300 years ago.

The exhibition gives an interesting snapshot of how life would have been for the garrison as well as the civilian population of Gibraltar during the early years of British occupation. The various rooms recall stories of life in Gibraltar during a time when sieges had blighted Gibraltar's population and hundreds of civilian as well as military personnel died from diseases like cholera and yellow fever. Look out for the various examples of graffiti drawn by soldiers on the walls of the building, some dating to as far back as 1726. Falling asleep while on duty was an offence punishable by execution, so sentries would often scratch pictures into the walls in order to stay awake. One particular piece of graffiti on the exterior wall of the main building is attributed to the aforementioned Sergeant Major Ince himself.

Gibraltar – A City Under Siege Exhibition

Willis's Magazine
Willis's Road
Gibraltar
Open: Monday-Sunday, 9.30am-7pm
Prices: Entry to the Upper Rock Nature Reserve costs £10 (adults) and £5 (children) and includes St Michael's Cave, City Under Siege Exhibition, the Moorish Castle and the Great Siege Tunnels.

Follow Willis's Road down past the **Moorish Castle's Tower of Homage**,

which can be entered via an entrance on the Tower's eastern wall.
The interior of the castle contains some well preserved medieval baths as well as various other remnants of Gibraltar's Muslim past. You can also make your way to the top of the tower where you can enjoy spectacular views over the Bay of Gibraltar and nearby Spain (for more information on the Moorish Castle see *Walk 2: Moorish Gibraltar*).

After exiting the castle, continue down on Willis's Road through the town area back to Main Street, where the walk ends.

– Walk 2 –
Moorish Gibraltar

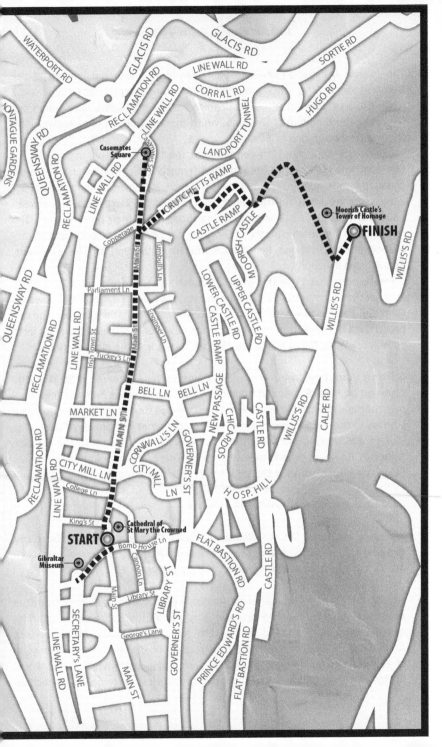

The Islamic occupation of Gibraltar began in 711 with the landing of the Berber general Tariq ibn-Ziyad, continuing almost uninterrupted until 1462 when Gibraltar was taken by Castilian forces. Just 30 years later would see the fall of the Kingdom of Granada, which marked the end of al-Andalus and the Islamic occupation of Europe.

It was not until the 12th century that the first extensive settlement on the Rock was built during the Almohad Dynasty (al-Muwahhidun). Gibraltar changed hands numerous times over the next 300 years among various Islamic sects including the Nasrids of Granada and the Merinids, who between 1309-1374 developed Gibraltar's fortifications along their present lines. The remnants of the medieval city of Gibraltar are revealed in contemporary archaeological excavations, beneath the modern British and, to a lesser extent, Spanish constructions.

Please note that I use the words "Moorish" and "Islamic" interchangeably as adjectives to collectively describe the various Muslim dynasties in power in Gibraltar. I appreciate that the word Moorish is somewhat antiquated and can be deemed misleading in certain contexts however it remains the term used colloquially as in for example the Moorish Castle and the Moorish Baths.

Getting your bearings: This walk begins at the Cathedral of St Mary the Crowned on Main Street and goes on to visit the Moorish Baths in the basement of the Gibraltar Museum. From here we visit the Moorish Castle complex starting in the area formerly known as La Barcina at present-day Casemates Square and making our way through the old town area up to the Castle's Tower of Homage, where the walk ends. There are various lunch options along the way at some of Gibraltar's Moroccan restaurants.

Length: Approximately 2km/1mi (3 hours)

*We start this walk at the Roman Catholic **Cathedral of St Mary the Crowned**, built on the site of Gibraltar's Great Mosque, supposedly the largest built in Gibraltar during the Almohad Dynasty.*

The Almohads were monotheistic fundamentalists who took over from the Almoravids as the ruling Empire in northern Africa and also went on to conquer most of Al-Andalus in the 12th century. It was the Almohad ruler, Abd-al-Mumin who ordered the construction of the Medinat al-fath (City of Faith) which is thought to be the first major settlement on the Rock. Al-Hayy Ya'is and Ahmad Ibn Baso, two of the most prominent architects of the Islamic world and who counted the Giralda tower in Seville and the Hassan Mosque in Rabat among their architectural credits, were brought in to lay-out and design the city. Apart from the Great Mosque, the City also comprised various defensive fortifications, a palace (possibly on the site of the Gibraltar Museum), a water-carrying system and a windmill at the summit of the Rock.

When the Spaniards captured Gibraltar they followed the common practice at the time of converting the Muslim places of worship into Roman Catholic cathedrals, much the same as occurred with the Giralda in Seville and the Mezquita in Córdoba. Initially much of the mosque's original structure was retained but the interior detail was thought to be an unworthy remnant of its idolatrous past and was soon discarded by the zealous Christian rulers. The small courtyard is all that remains of the Mosque's larger court, which was once said to have been adorned with rows of orange trees. In recent years, orange trees have been planted on Main Street outside the Cathedral to commemorate this once famous courtyard. The church was eventually consecrated as Gibraltar's parish church and took the name Santa Maria la Coronada y San Bernardo before being demolished by the Spanish to be re-built in a Gothic Style. The Catholic Monarchs' coat of arms can barely be made out on the courtyard's eastern wall. The Building would have a further facelift after the Great Siege of Gibraltar when the Spanish-built structure was destroyed, ironically perhaps, by Spanish cannon shot. When the building was rebuilt in its present style, its façade was moved to its present position in order to straighten Main Street.

Opposite the Cathedral, by the statue that commemorates the Royal Engineers, is a narrow alley known as Bomb House Lane, which leads to the **Gibraltar Museum**. The Museum is built on the site of what is thought to have been the palace of the Merinid Governor of Gibraltar during the early 14th century, contemporaneously with the Moorish Castle's **Tower of Homage**. The palace would probably have been an elaborate construction and its private bath house, which can still be seen in the basement of the museum, is one of the most well-preserved examples of its

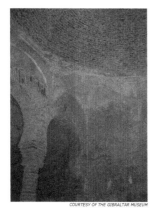

COURTESY OF THE GIBRALTAR MUSEUM

kind in Europe. During the Moorish occupation, baths were often attached to a mosque serving the dual function of cleansing both body and soul. Public baths were far more than just bathing establishments, they were also barber shops and massage parlours where the men of the town would relax and also do a spot of networking. Though these baths were private, there is no doubt that there would have been certain social rituals attached to them and one can almost envisage the governor discussing politics or business within them in the presence of visiting dignitaries.

The so-called **Moorish Baths** are made up of three chambers, which operated by way of an underground network of canals that circulate hot air. The first chamber as you enter is the al-bayt al-barid or the "cool room", which contained a cold water basin and star-shaped openings in the roof that not only provided light but were also essential architecturally as they reduced the weight of the thick insulated ceilings. The next room, the al-bayt al-maslaj or the vestibule, is where the bather would undress and you will note the niches on the walls where bathers would store their street clothes and shoes. The third room is probably the most ornate of all the rooms with its domed ceiling and its tremendously ornate stone arches and columns. This was the al-bayt al-wastani also known as the tepidarium offering the bather a constant radiant heat from the walls and floor. The final smaller room is the al-bayt al-sajun or "hot room" where underground fires heated both the waters and the floor. A further two (inaccessible) rooms, probably the boiler room and a store room lie adjacent to the hot room forming part of a more extensive complex of baths of which only the abovementioned rooms survive.

The Gibraltar Museum

18/20 Bomb House Lane
Gibraltar
Tel. +350 200 74298
Fax +350 200 79158
E-mail enquiries@museum.gib.gi
Open: Monday-Friday, 10am-6pm (last entry 5.30pm); Saturday,
10am-2pm (last entry 1.30pm) Sundays: closed
Prices: £2 (adults), £1 (children, aged 12 and under), under 5s: free.

Before leaving the Museum complex, it is worth stopping to see the trenches in the Museum's garden, which, during an archaeological dig, unearthed various vestiges of Gibraltar's Moorish past including a well built during the Merinid Dynasty.

The Governor's Palace had extensive grounds to its south and this encompassed the areas of the Museum's garden and the swimming pool of the adjacent Bristol Hotel. In addition, the dig also unearthed relics dating back to the Almohad Dynasty demonstrating that this area may have been in use since the days of the Medinat al-fath. As a result of these findings, the Museum's garden was renamed in honour of Abd-al-Mumin, the founder of what may have been Gibraltar's first major settlement.

Return to Main Street and turn left, walking north towards Casemates Square.

There are various restaurants specializing in Moroccan cuisiine on the Rock. If you make your way up Cannon Lane in the direction of the Eliott Hotel you will find 'Marakesh Restaurant' on Governor's Parade which specializes in tagines and couscous, served at reasonable prices. There is a further Moroccan restaurant closer to Casemates Square on Turnbulls Lane, behind the Venture Inn pub. The 'Moroccan Restaurant' serves arguably the best pinchitos (beef

COURTESY OF THE GIBRALTAR MUSEUM

and chicken skewers) in town, albeit in shabby surroundings.

*Arriving at Casemates Square make your way to the Little Rock bar, outside of which can be found part of the foundations of an original **Moorish Galley House** or Atarazana built under the Merinid leader Abu l'Hasan.*

The medieval harbour, located approximately where the Square now stands was constructed within the original city walls and the Water Gate through which boats would enter the harbour was positioned near the present site of Grand Casemates

Gate. Although very little remains to show what this area might have looked like during the early Moorish occupation of the Rock, the foundations of the Galley House at least give some indication of how the area might have been used during this time (the Moorish Galley House is described in more detail in *Walk 4: Naval Gibraltar*).

Looking up towards the Rock from Casemates you will notice the series of buildings and walls known as the Moorish Castle. These are what remain of a larger Castle complex which, as the town got larger, eventually extended downwards from its highest point at the Tower of Homage to encompass the area of Casemates Square. Nearest the Tower are the Inner and Outer Keeps followed by the Qassabah (or Kasbah), which is where the Moorish Castle housing estate now stands. The Castle complex would have extended west towards the sea through an area later known as the Villa Vieja, whose western boundary lay approximately at Crutchett's Ramp. At the southern end of the Square, some red telephone boxes mark the position of a 14th-century wall that was built during the Merinid Dynasty. The remains of this wall were unearthed during an archaeological excavation and although these were subsequently covered when Main Street was repaved, the dig also revealed the remains of a gate in this area that controlled entry into the area later known as La Barcina.

Make your way back onto Main Street where you will soon see the Venture Inn pub on your left hand side. A small alleyway adjacent to this public house leads to Turnbull's Lane where Morocco Restaurant offers perhaps the most genuine experience of Moroccan cuisine on the Rock.

This is the oldest eatery specializing in Moroccan cuisine in Gibraltar and the beef and chicken pinchitos (meat skewers) are among the best you will find this side of the Strait.

*Returning to the Venture Inn, begin your ascent of the adjacent **Crutchett's Ramp**.*

Many of Gibraltar's hills are known as ramps, which is actually a throwback to when they were originally constructed as gun-ramps for transporting weapons and ammunition to batteries. The summit of the Ramp is an ideal vantage point for examining the rear of the 6th and 7th Crutchett's Batteries, which extend down en Crémaillère beyond the Castle Batteries from the Tower of Homage. Although these batteries and the walls connecting them are mainly British-built, the remnants of the anterior Spanish and Moorish structures can still be seen in places along the current lines.

*Follow Demaya's Ramp, named after a rich merchant who lived in the area, up to the Road to the Lines. Turn right and follow the route around the modern buildings up to the high wall that marks the eastern extreme of the Villa Vieja. Follow the path of the wall to your left as you skirt around the rear of the buildings until you reach a steep set of downward steps. After descending a few steps, turn right and cut through the wall. On your left hand side, a sealed metal fence leads to the area known as the **Northern Defences**.*

During the Middle Ages this area, which was later to become a series of tiered batteries, provided the main land-approach into Gibraltar. The remains of the **Gate of Granada** can be seen in close proximity on the other side of the fence. This was the main entrance into the city during the 14th-century Merinid occupation of Gibraltar and the remains of two of its pillars give some indication of the original size of the gate. The Gate, which faces in the direction of Granada just as the Puerta de Africa at the city's southern extreme points towards Africa, also reveals the important connection between Gibraltar and the Kingdom of Granada during the Merinid dynasty.

Continue to ascend further into the former Qassabah, the remnants of which have sadly now been largely buried under the Moorish Castle housing estate.

This area would originally have housed the Governor's Palace and was also said to have contained fantastic gardens and vineyards as well as woodland where the governor would have hunted deer and wild boar.

*Follow the route between the buildings in the direction of the Moorish Castle Social Club. A gate is cut into the wall adjacent to the club and a flight of stairs on the exterior of the wall leads to the important East Gate, also know as the **Moorish Gate House**, which is considered to be the oldest man-made structure in Gibraltar.*

The Gate House was made up of two towers that controlled a vaulted entranceway, which offered extra protection from enemy attackers. The Gate House was built during the Nasrid Dynasty and an inscription above the door (in Arabic and which is no longer visible) once recorded a dedication to Yusef I, the Sultan of Granada, as well as mentioning the year 744 as being the year the original castle structure was completed. A later inscription denotes the year 1789 and it was probably around this time that the British modified the Gate House for use as a powder magazine. The building's conical roof was also added during this period. Although further modern alterations have been made to the gate's structure, it is still possible to appreciate the typically Moorish stonework and architecture on either side of the gate's main entranceway as well as on its adjoining curtain walls.

The Gate House is one of four towers on the south-east wall and following the wall in the direction of the Tower of Homage you will soon see another of these towers, a slender circular tower constructed en bec, which refers to its pointed or beak-like projection. This tower would have been built in this manner as a means of strengthening its base, and judging by the style and materials used it is likely to be a more modern structure than the Gate House.

It is interesting to note the different layers of construction that can be seen on the curtain walls denoting the varying building methods employed during different eras. The older parts of the wall were constructed using tapia,

a rammed earth mortar mixed with lime and gravel and finished with still visible lines of white limewash, which were designed to simulate ordinary coursed masonry. This area of the Castle was until very recently used as Gibraltar's prison and there is a square tower further up the curtain wall near what used to be the prison's main entrance. However you will be able to see a further square tower further up the curtain wall near the prison's entrance as you continue your climb towards the Tower of Homage.

*Continue to ascend via Tankerville Road between numerous modern build-
ings and you will eventually find your way onto Willis's Road, where you
should turn left and continue up to the **Tower of Homage***.

The Tower is undoubtedly one of Gibraltar's most famous landmarks and still
proudly flies the British flag from its battlements just as it did when Admiral
Rooke captured the Rock in 1704. Despite its iconic status, it is hard to know
exactly when the original castle structure was built, with some historians
speculating that construction commenced not long after Tariq's landing at
the beginning of the 8th century. This would probably make Gibraltar's castle
the first Moorish fortification to be built on European soil. A tower located
approximately in the vicinity of the present Tower of Homage would certainly
have existed around 1160 and this was itself purportedly built on the site of
a former construction. The 1160 structure was badly damaged in the early
14th century and was re-built in its present form around this time by the
Merinids. Further alterations to the Tower, which was known as the Calahorra
during Spanish times, took place when the Nasrids of Granada took over
Gibraltar around 1374.

A close inspection of the Tower's eastern wall betrays both its age as
well as the extensive damage it has received during the numerous sieges
Gibraltar has withheld during the Tower's long life. A plaque near the Brit-

ish 32-pounder cannon on Queen Charlotte's Battery describes some of the attacks inflicted on the castle, including the siege of 1333 by Alfonso XI of Castille where the attacking forces were said to have positioned siege machines high up on the Rock above the Tower.

The white patches on the exterior of the Tower of Homage are the remnants of the lime whitewash that once covered the whole tower and gave it its previous name of La Torre Blanca or the White Tower. You should also look out for a bricked-up archway about half-way up the eastern wall, which would have been the Tower's main entrance before the present entrance was cut and was probably accessed via a wooden staircase. The merlons visible on the right hand side of the Tower's eastern wall and similar merlons along the summit of the tower are later additions, probably built by the British.

The current entrance to the Tower at the bottom right corner of the eastern wall sports a heavily spring-loaded door to keep the Barbary macaques out, so you should look over your shoulder as you enter the Tower to make sure you are not being followed. A modern metal staircase that has replaced the original stone staircase leads downwards into the Castle's inner keep although this area is inaccessible since parts of this are still used as Gibraltar's civil prison.

Follow the steps up to the first floor which contains a stunningly preserved medieval bathhouse not dissimilar to the type found in the basement of the Gibraltar Museum.

Many of the features of the baths mirror the Museum's bathhouse such as the high vaulted ceilings and star-shaped cavities that allow light into the rooms. There is also a series of underground canals for circulating hot air and a furnace room adjacent to the dressing area, with blackened walls that betray the room's former use.

The large room at the south-eastern end of the building may have been living quarters for the governor although it is unlikely that it would have been his permanent residence and he would probably only have retreated to the castle during times of crisis. The small prayer room is probably the most impressive room in the Tower with its ornate ceiling mouldings. This was converted into a Christian chapel by the Spanish and the remains of Don Enrique de Guzman were said to have been laid to rest here. The sealed archway at the far end of the room was the former entry to the Tower via a timber walkway and you can still see centuries-old graffiti, scratched into the wall by the sentries who guarded the gate down the years.

Finally, ascend the final set of stairs to the roof of the castle where you can enjoy spectacular views over the Bay and town of Gibraltar and, on a clear day, for miles up the Spanish coastline. The Tower of Homage is the largest remaining Moorish tower in the Iberian Peninsular and it is here, at its summit, that this walk ends.

Moorish Castle
Willis's Road
Gibraltar
Open: Monday-Sunday, 9.30am-7pm
Prices: Entry to the Upper Rock Nature Reserve costs £10 (adults) and £5 (children) and includes St Michael's Cave, City Under Siege Exhibition, the Moorish Castle and the Great Siege Tunnels.

– Walk 3 –
Gibraltar from
North to South

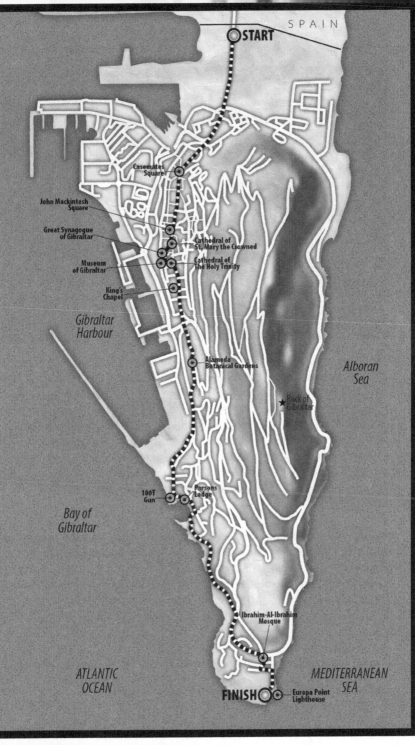

Gibraltar is about 3mi (4.8km) in length from the land border with Spain to Europa Point and has a total circumference of about 7mi (11.2km). There have been times during Gibraltar's history that, due to high sea levels, Gibraltar has actually been an island disconnected from the Iberian mainland. In fact in 1655, Edward Montagu the First Earl of Sandwich suggested to Oliver Cromwell that if Gibraltar was taken, the most efficient way of securing it would be to dig a canal across the isthmus, cutting Gibraltar away from the mainland. The capture of Gibraltar by the British was not to occur for another 50 years, but in any event the plan to build the canal was never seen through.

Getting your bearings: This walk begins on the Gibraltarian side of the land border with Spain. You will be walking from the northernmost point of Gibraltar to Europa Point, which is its southernmost tip. The city of Gibraltar lies on Gibraltar's west coast and the Rock itself will remain on your left hand side, with the city walls and the ocean on your right (west) until you reach Europa. From here you can then either catch a bus back to town or travel back by foot.

Length: Approximately 5km/3mi, or 10km/6mi if you choose to walk rather than take the bus back from Europa Point (4 hours/6 hours)

The position of the land border between Gibraltar and Spain has been a bone of contention between the British and Spanish governments for many years. Prior to 1909 only a line of sentries, positioned close to where the frontier fence is located today, divided the narrow strip of land that connects Gibraltar to mainland Spain (the isthmus). In order to reduce the costs of patrolling the area, the British decided to build a fence on the Gibraltar side of the old line of sentry posts. The original fence was built of steel and was 2m high with three strands of barbed wire adding a further 0.5m to the fence's height. This was not to the liking of the Spanish authorities but due to Britain's might and Spain's relative weakness at the time, there was very little they could have conceivably done to remedy this situation. The present fence, although of similar un-climbable height with barbed wire at its crown, is now made of PVC-coated chain link fencing mesh separated by Y-shaped concrete posts.

Just a few metres from the frontier fence you will see **Gibraltar's airport terminal**. Located about 500m from Gibraltar's city centre, there is no airport terminal in the world situated closer to the city that it serves. In 2007 work began on the construction of a new two-storey, 20,000-m-sq airport terminal, four times the size of the earlier one. The new, highly controversial air terminal was finally completed in 2011 and became fully operational in 2012. Prior to the advent of air flight, the area where the airport terminal and runway presently stand had been a large open recreational area used for training purposes by the garrison. It was also home to Gibraltar's own racecourse, built during the Napoleonic Wars, and said to have brought together the local and military communities on both sides of the frontier. Excellent black and white photographs of the racecourse and the surrounding area can be seen in the airport's departure lounge.

In the 1930s, the need to provide air defence for the Rock became more apparent and the isthmus was identified as the only flat area in Gibraltar suitable for creating a runway. The problem was that there were questions over whether this area had been properly ceded to the British under the Treaty of Utrecht. Legal advice was sought on the implications of building the runway on this area, but contrary to the advice given, it was decided to use the isthmus as an emergency landing field. The necessary preparations were made to the ground and a landing area that traversed the centre of the racecourse was declared useable on March 10, 1936. The landing ground was controlled by the Navy and during the following years there was an increased volume of aircraft landings, culminating in 1941 with the extension of the runway into the sea. In 1942 Gibraltar became the staging ground for Operation Torch, the Allied invasion of North Africa that was overseen by US general Dwight D.

Eisenhower, who set up his headquarters for the operation on the Rock. During November of that year, the now completed runway assembled over 400 fighter planes, mainly Spitfires and Hurricaines which were dispatched from Gibraltar to the North African front.

The runway offers a great view of the Rock's precipitous **North Face**, whose natural and insurmountable protective wall has been extensively galleried with embrasures for mounting guns. From the runway it is also possible to see the barrels of two of the 5.25-inch AA guns positioned on **Princess Anne's Battery**, a shelf of rock about two-thirds of the way up the Rock. This is one of the Rock's main defensive fortifications and is the only intact battery of this type anywhere in the world (Princess Anne's Battery is described in more detail in *Walk 1: Pre-Twentieth Century British Military History*).

*Once you have crossed the runway, continue up to the sundial roundabout where, on the left hand side of the road you will see the **Cross of Sacrifice** and **Gibraltar Memorial**.*

This memorial stands in a triangular site and commemorates by name 91 airmen and soldiers who were buried at sea during World War II. The names of 7 servicemen who died when the SS Woodfield was sunk by an Austrian submarine on November 9, 1915 were added to the cenotaph after the original memorial to these men, which stood in the North Front cemetery, was demolished. The Cross is made of Cornish granite and the Gibraltar Memorial is made of local limestone with Cornish granite panels. A ceremony of

remembrance is held here once a year on the second Sunday of November (Remembrance Sunday).
Continue your path along Winston Churchill Avenue between the two housing estates.

This area has undergone an enormous transformation over the last three centuries. The width of the isthmus used to taper inwards creating a narrow approach to the northern part of the town, which was flanked on one side by the sea that would have reached the western side of Winston Churchill Avenue. On the other side, on the site of the Laguna housing estate was a low marshy area, or morass, which was flooded in 1762 and came to be known as the inundation or the lagoon—giving the housing estate its present name. Together, the sea and the inundation made any land attack on Gibraltar very difficult as the only land route to the town was via a narrow causeway that was heavily safeguarded by the Northern Defences, a series of layered batteries that you can see shelved on the north-western side of the Rock. A minefield was laid in the area in front of the Landport in the 18th century and a network of tunnels was excavated through the Rock providing further embrasures on which to place guns. These embrasures, positioned intermittently along the north and north-west faces of the Rock are clearly visible from the runway and along Winston Churchill Avenue.

Carry on walking beyond the pedestrian crossing, and take the first left turning after the Eurolife building, taking you past a skate-park on your right hand side up to **Landport Gate** *(The Landport Defences and Gate are described in more detail in* Walk 7: Defensive Fortifications of Gibraltar*). Cross the timber drawbridge and walk through the gate along the tunnel, followed by a further tunnel that crosses through Casemates Barracks to* **Grand Casemates Square***.*

The Square was built as a military parade ground and continues to be used for this purpose even today, although not as regularly. It also famously played host to Gibraltar's last public hanging in 1864. The square is now a busy commercial area and a popular meeting point for locals. At night, particularly during the summer months, the square comes alive with revellers spilling out of the pubs and clubs that surround it. Every Saturday at 12 noon, a historical re-enactment parade known as History Alive takes place, where a troop of soldiers in 18th-century period uniform march from Bomb House Lane to Casemates where they carry out a "Ceremony of the Keys" routine before marching back up Main Street to the Cathedral of St Mary the Crowned.

There is a Tourist Office located on the eastern side of the square beside Grand Casemates Gate, which was built on the site of the old Water Gate, from where the medieval inhabitants of the town would have launched their galleys into the sea. The Tourist Office offers an ideal vantage point to view the surroundings, starting off with the Casemates Barracks, which lie parallel to Grand Battery and dominate the northern end of the Square. These were originally designed in 1770 by Chief Engineer William Green as bombproof accommodation for soldiers but were not completed until 1817. These former barracks are now a large arcade with bars and restaurants, niche boutiques and an art gallery. Despite its renovation in the mid-1990s, most of the units retain many of the building's original features.

The area near Casemates Square is where the foundations were laid by the first Moorish occupiers of the Rock and probably formed part of the first large settlement in Gibraltar. Of particular note is the original **Moorish**

Galley House or *Atarazana* which can be seen at the northern end of the square outside the Little Rock restaurant (The Galley House and medieval dockyard are described in more detail in *Walk 4: Naval Gibraltar* and the Square's Moorish origins are covered in *Walk 2: Moorish Gibraltar*). In addition to the replica Koehler Gun that stands in front of the Tourist Office (described in more detail in *Walk 5: The Guns of Gibraltar*), there is a **Statue of a Soldier of the Gibraltar Defence Force** (GDF) at the southern end of the Square. The GDF paraded for the first time on the April 28, 1939 and is a forerunner of what is now the Royal Gibraltar Regiment. Composed of local volunteers, the GDF served side-by-side with the standard units of the Garrison and this statue symbolizes Gibraltar's role in the defence of the Rock during World War II. Casemates (or the nearby public market) is a good place to have a breakfast of churros, a traditional fried-dough snack that is extremely popular with Gibraltarians.

A set of red telephone boxes mark the beginning of Main Street.

Sometimes called Calle Real, this is Gibraltar's main shopping and commercial hub, which cuts through the centre of what was Gibraltar's old town and runs parallel to the town's western line of defences. The International Commercial Centre (ICC) stands on the location of the old naval yard, which used to be known as the White Convent and housed various naval warehouses and a cooperage for the storing of water casks. The small lane on your right hand side leading from Main Street to Irish Town is called Cooperage Lane commemorating its former use. At first observation Main Street may appear to mirror the style of many typical British pedestrian shopping avenues and indeed the many Georgian constructions along its length verify this contention. However looking above street level, the elaborate wrought-iron balconies and the many tiled façades paint a vastly different picture, as do the wooden shutters that adorn almost every window.

Continuing your route south on Main Street, you will soon see Gibraltar's main Post Office on your right hand side.

The post office was established in Gibraltar in 1857, when the Overland Post Office and the Packet Agency were merged under the control of Britain's Postmaster General. Plans were soon adopted to build a new post office building and on September 1, 1858 the Gibraltar Post Office at 104 Main Street was inaugurated, just a few months after British postage stamps were first placed on sale in Gibraltar. After a little less than half the length of Main Street, you should turn right into **John Macintosh Square**, known nowadays as the Piazza. This Square has undergone various refurbishments and name changes throughout the years but few will deny its importance as one of the most prominent squares and meeting places for Gibraltarians. The Piazza used to be called Commercial Square and during this time hosted a daily flea market and public auctions, inspiring its other colloquial nickname el Martillo meaning literally "the hammer". In 1940 the Square's name was changed once again to honour the memory of local philanthropist John Mackintosh, whose bust overlooks the square.

The square is flanked on either side by two of Gibraltar's most important buildings. **The House of Assembly**, the front of which overlooks Main Street and was built in 1817 as the Exchange, and **Commercial Library** built by then Governor Sir George Don, whose own bust can be seen on the upper part of the building from Main Street. The building was funded by public subscription and a list of the subscribers can still be seen in the building's lobby. After becoming Gibraltar's Commercial Library, the building was damaged by fire in 1919 and large parts of it were re-built in a different style to the original building. In 1950 the building became Gibraltar's Legislative Council and then in 1969, it became the House of Assembly, which was Gibraltar's equivalent to the Houses of Parliament. In 2006 it was finally renamed the Gibraltar Parliament.

Opposite the House of Assembly is the building known today as the **City Hall**. This building was built in 1819 as a private mansion for Aaron Nunez Cardozo, a wealthy Jewish merchant who settled in Gibraltar. After Cardozo died in 1834 the building's use changed several times including its time as the exclusive Club House Hotel. It was also temporarily the residence of the Duke of Connaught, Queen Victoria's son, who was stationed in Gibraltar in the early 1900s and began to be known as Connaught House. The building was eventually sold to the Gibraltar Government in 1920 for around £40,000 and became the offices of the newly formed City Council, adopting its current name. A plaque on the exterior of the building details its recent history (further information on the City Hall and in particular its links to Admiral Nelson are described in *Walk 4: Naval Gibraltar*).

Before returning to Main Street, it is worth noting the Victorian police station on Irish Town at the northern end of the Square. This building was constructed in 1864 during the governorship of General Sir William Codrington and was the main headquarters of the Royal Gibraltar Police until this was relocated to the police station at New Mole House. The Gibraltar Police was formed on June 25, 1830, making it the oldest Commonwealth police service, and was granted the Royal accolade by the Queen in 1992.

Returning to Main Street and continuing south you will soon reach the **Cathedral of St Mary the Crowned**, *which was built on the site of what was, during the Muslim occupation of the Rock, Gibraltar's main mosque.*

When Gibraltar came under Spanish rule, Queen Isabella ordered that it be rebuilt as a church in a Gothic style, with a typical high dock and bell tower. The structure survived the British conquest but suffered extensive damage during frequent attacks and particularly during the Great Siege. It was once again rebuilt in 1790 during Sir Robert Boyd's second tenure as the Governor of Gibraltar. It was at this time that its main façade was repositioned to where it is today in an effort to straighten Main Street. Although remnants of the Spanish structure still remain, numerous refurbishments have meant that the Cathedral as it stands today differs greatly from that which was built under Queen Isabella's rule.

Entering the Cathedral via the side entrance (to the left of the Cathedral's main entrance), you find yourself in what remains of the courtyard once known as the Patio de los Naranjos (Courtyard of the Orange Trees). Set into the wall on the court's eastern wall you can still make out the coat-of-arms of Queen Isabella and King Ferdinand of Spain. The patio also leads to the Chapel of Our Lady of Lourdes and the archway that forms the entrance to the chapel was part of the original Spanish church, giving some indication of the church's original height and shape. The interior of the chapel was built in the late 19th century by then Bishop, Gonzalo Canilla and his Episcopal seal adorns the front of the altar.

Entering the Cathedral's main building via the side door, you will be immediately drawn to the spectacularly high Italian marble altar which was said to have been built in a style similar to the altar of St Peter's Basilica in Rome.

It had originally been constructed for use in a church in South America, but when the ship carrying it sank in the Bay of Gibraltar, the altar was salvaged and donated to the Cathedral. There are statues of the Four Evangelists on the altar and relics of the saints dating back to the Spanish period can be found at the base of each statue. To the left of the high altar is the altar of St Mary the Crowned which is adorned with a statue of St Mary. The original statue that gave the church its name can only be viewed by private appointment as it is located within the Church's sacristy. There are various memorial tablets on the floor of the sanctuary and throughout the church. On the right hand side of the high altar, in front of the Altar of the Blessed Sacrament, a memorial honours Monsignor Narciso Pallares, a member of the local clergy who was murdered in the Cathedral by a madman in 1885. The Cathedral's stained-glass windows are mainly modern having been shattered when the RFA Bedenham, a naval

 armament carrier, exploded while docked in Gibraltar in 1951.

Cathedral of Saint Mary the Crowned
215 Main Street
Gibraltar
Tel. +350 200 76688
Fax +350 200 43112
E-mail cathedral@gibtelecom.net
Mass held: Monday-Friday, 7.30am, 9.15am,
12.25pm, 6.15pm
Saturday, 6.30pm (family mass)
Sunday. 9am, 10.30am, 12pm, 6.30pm

Opposite the Cathedral there is a plinth with a life-sized Statue Commemorating the Royal Engineers and their services to Gibraltar. Though military engineers have always served in the armies of the Crown, the origins of the modern corps of Royal Engineers have their roots in the Soldier Artificer Company, which was established for service in Gibraltar in 1782 as the first non-commissioned military engineers. The Royal Engineers in their various forms are responsible for many of Gibraltar's fortifications with their most noteworthy legacy being the labyrinthine network of tunnels through the Rock, which have had such a pivotal role in Gibraltar's defence through the years. The tunnels are an amazing feat of engineering and were described by the Duc de Crillon, who commanded the defeated French and Spanish attackers at the Great Siege, as being "worthy of the Romans".

*Taking a diversion off Main Street once again, down Bomb House Lane, which lies directly behind the Royal Engineers statue, you will find the **Great Synagogue of Gibraltar**.*

This was the first synagogue to operate on the Iberian Peninsula after the expulsion of the Jews from Spain in 1492. It was founded in 1724 by Isaac

Nieto on a plot of land granted to the Jews of Gibraltar by then governor Brigadier General Richard Kane although much of the present structure was built in the early 19th century. Next to the Great Synagogue is the Gibraltar Museum, which houses some of the most important objects relating to Gibraltar's history ranging from Palaeolithic and Bronze Age artefacts to 20th-century prints and photographs. The museum was officially opened in 1930 by then governor General Sir Alexander Godley and the building had previously been home to Gibraltar's principal ordinance officer. The patio, which can be accessed free of charge, features the archaeological remains of a 16th-century Spanish Aqueduct that carried water to a cistern within the museum building as well as some earlier Muslim structures.

Entry to the museum is highly recommended, particularly considering its low admission price of only £2 for adults. A short video is played near the museum's entrance giving an excellent précis on Gibraltar's history in under 15 minutes. You will probably need at least another 1.5 hours to make the most of the rest of the museum's displays. The exhibitions do not always follow a chronological theme, giving the museum a slightly haphazard feel at times as you jump forward and back through different periods of Gibraltar's history. Particularly worthy of mention is the scale model of the Rock, which provides a thoroughly detailed three-dimensional view of Gibraltar as it was during the late 19th century. The model was one of two built in 1868 by Sappers Williams and McLellan from a survey made by Lieutenant Charles Warren of the Royal Engineers who also oversaw the model's completion. The complex of medieval baths situated in the basement of the building are undoubtedly the jewel in the Museum's crown and represent one of the most complete examples of baths of this type that can be found in Europe today (these are described in more detail in Walk 2: Moorish Gibraltar).

The Gibraltar Museum

18/20 Bomb House Lane
Gibraltar
Tel. +350 200 74298
Fax +350 200 79158
E-mail enquiries@museum.gib.gi
Open: Monday-Friday, 10am-6pm (last entry 5.30pm); Saturday, 10am-2pm (last entry 1.30pm); Sundays: closed
Prices: £2 (adults), £1 (children, aged 12 and under), under 5s: free.

Continue along Bomb House Lane past the Deanery, the official residence of

the Dean of Gibraltar, in the direction of the Bristol Hotel until you arrive at
*the **Cathedral of the Holy Trinity**.*

When it was built in 1838, the Church of the Holy Trinity replaced King's Chapel as the main place of Anglican worship in Gibraltar. It was not until 1842 that the Holy Trinity was raised to Cathedral status and became the central location of what is now known as the Diocese in Europe. This Diocese encompasses all Anglican chaplaincies in southern Europe and east up to the Caspian Sea meaning that due to his many commitments the Anglican Bishop of Gibraltar will rarely be able to stay on the Rock for more than a few days at a time. The first Bishop of Gibraltar was George Tomlinson (from 1842-1863).

The Cathedral contains tributes to many well known Anglicans who have lived on the Rock. The main doors, for example, are dedicated to the memory of Bishop Horsley. Visitors should also note the Lady Chapel with its ornamental door and impressive bronze altar. The tombs in the chancel are those of Sir George Don who ordered the building of the Cathedral but died before it was completed, as well as those of Lady Houston, the wife of Don's successor and Dean Govett, the first Dean of Gibraltar.

The most impressive stained glass window is the one located at the eastern side of the Cathedral and which can be viewed from Main Street or Cathedral Square. Like those of the Cathedral of St Mary the Crowned, this is not the original window, which was shattered in 1951 when the Royal Fleet Auxiliary RFA Bendenham blew up in the harbour. The Cathedral's main altar is also worthy of note. Two additional marble slabs were added in the 1960s but the original altar contains carvings in an Islamic style, following a theme used throughout the Cathedral in commemoration of Gibraltar's seven centuries of Islamic rule. A plaque was recently added to commemorate the visit of

former Archbishop of Canterbury, Dr George Carey.

Cathedral of the Holy Trinity
Cathedral Square
Gibraltar
Tel. +350 200 75745
Fax +350 200 78463
E-mail anglicangib@gibtelecom.net
Morning Prayer held daily at 9.30am,
10am on Sundays; evening prayer
daily at 6pm; sung Eucharist held
on Sundays at 10.30am

Returning to Main Street, continue south until you reach the Gibraltar Court building recognizable by a small landscaped garden at the front of the building.

Gibraltar has a Magistrates' Court and a Supreme Court that has criminal jurisdiction comparable to that of the English Crown Court and civil jurisdiction resembling that of the English High Court. The court building was built in 1830 and was originally fronted by large Grecian columns before taking its present form in an 1888 restoration. One of the most famous cases heard in these courts was that of the sailing vessel Marie Celeste whose crew mysteriously disappeared in the Atlantic Ocean in 1872. John Lennon and Yoko Ono also famously married at the Registry Office in this building on March 20, 1969. Opposite the Courts is the Gibraltar Bookshop (300 Main Street, opening hours Monday-Friday 10.30am-6.30pm), which is of note for its standing as Gibraltar's oldest book shop, as well as the fine selection of local-interest books on its shelves.

Continuing south on Main Street you will soon see King's Chapel on the right hand side of the road which was the first place of Anglican worship in Gibraltar.

This charming chapel originally built in 1560 lies adjacent to the governor of Gibraltar's official residence on the Rock, which is known locally as the Convent after a Convent of Franciscan Friars that existed on this site prior to the British arrival on the Rock. Finally, opposite the Convent and flanked on either side by well-polished brass cannons is the Convent Guard Room where a Changing of the Guard ceremony is held daily (Kings Chapel and the Convent are described in more detail in *Walk 1: Pre-Twentieth Century British Military History)*.

Kings Chapel
Main Street, Gibraltar
Open to the Public: Monday-Saturday,

9.30am-5.30pm.
Mass is held on Saturday at 5.45pm (Roman Catholic Mass) and Sunday at 10.30am (Anglican Mass)
Continue along the exterior wall of the Convent's gardens, which extend south along Main Street until you reach the John Mackintosh Hall.

This local cultural centre was built in the 1960s, on the site of the former military Grand Stores that had to be demolished after also being badly damaged during the Bedenham's explosion in 1951. The John Mackintosh Hall is home to Gibraltar's library and its Gallery and Exhibition Halls regularly host exhibitions by local artists. Next to the John Mackintosh Hall is Inces Hall, a theatre housed in an old armoury building built in the mid 18th century and is named after Sergeant Major Ince, the architect of the Great Siege Tunnels. Opposite Ince's Hall there is a stone archway which, contrary to what is written on the adjoining red plaque, is actually all that remains of the Hermitage of Nuestra Senora del Rosario, which used to be located in the Villa Vieja part of the city above Casemates.

Before reaching the curtain wall that marks the southern end of Gibraltar's old town, you will note an elaborately painted 19th-century, 18-ton 10-inch Rifled Muzzle Loader (RML) cannon with a three-cannon insignia on its barrel.

Next to the cannon, there is a sentry box with a waxwork sentry wearing the 19th-century uniform of the Kings Own Scottish Rifles. A second model in a sentry box built into the **Charles V Wall** and partially obscured behind a modern fountain wears the old uniform of the 28th Gloucestershire Regiment. During the Moorish occupation of the Rock, a walled structure of some description would have stood on the location of the present wall, however the vastly improved Spanish wall dates back to 1550 and was designed by Italian engineer Giovanni Battista Calvi.

The wall enhanced Gibraltar's southern line of defence from attack by Barbary pirates including those under the command of the infamous Barbarossa who looted the city and enslaved many of its inhabitants. The lower end of the wall cannot be traversed but the upper end was refurbished and offers an alternative walking route from the area known as the Apes Den to the summit of the Rock.

There are three gates cut into the wall. The first and original gate, the smallest of the three, bears the date 1552 and Gibraltar's crest as well as the coats of arms of Charles V and that of the Marquis of Medina Sidonia who was governor at the time the gate was cut. This gate was originally known as Puerta de Africa or Door of Africa and on either side of Charles V's coat of arms (he was actually Charles I of Spain) are pillars with the words non plus ultra, which was his personal motto and bears reference to Gibraltar as one of the pillars of Hercules. According to myth, the Pillars bore this warning, which translates as "nothing further beyond" to warn sailors not to venture any further.

A second opening was cut in 1883 when major improvements were made to the wall and the Royal coat of arms of Queen Victoria and General Sir John Adye are carved in stone above the arch. The final and largest gate is known as Referendum Gate, commemorating Gibraltar's first referendum held on September 10, 1967. The Naval Picket House, which was located on the interior of the wall where the gate is now located, was demolished when this gate was cut in 1967. On the exterior of the wall on this location was an extension of the Southport Ditch, which was backfilled when the Referendum Gate was opened. Adjacent to the exterior of the wall on the eastern side of Southport Ditch is the **Trafalgar Cemetery** where lie the remains of military personnel who served on the Rock including some who died in the Battle of Trafalgar (the Trafalgar Cemetery is described in more detail in *Walk 4: Naval Gibraltar*).

Beyond Charles V Gate and Trafalgar Cemetery is the Grand Parade, which marks the beginning of Gibraltar's South District. Once an assembly and parade ground used for ceremonial occasions, the Grand Parade is now a large free-of-charge parking area and home to the Cable Car base station. The Grand Parade provides entry to the **Alameda Botanical Gardens** either via George Don Gate at the southern end of the Grand Parade or through the walk-way on the eastern side of the Parade behind the two large 10-inch, 18-ton RML guns.

The Gardens were opened in 1816 by the then lieutenant-governor, General Sir George Don, who considered at the time that Gibraltar had very few areas of public recreation. Nowadays the Gardens are owned by the Gibraltar Government but run privately, and there is even an open air theatre that hosts variety shows and live concerts. There is also a small wildlife park with parrots and other exotic birds as well as land tortoises and various species of ape that have been confiscated from illegal traders and cannot be let back into the wild. The wildlife park has a small gift shop that sells refreshments and souvenirs.

The Gardens are deceivingly large with a seemingly endless maze of interconnecting paths and flower beds sculpted from native Jurassic limestone and tinted by the famous red sand common to the area. The **Eliott Memorial** at the summit of the Heathfield Steps was commissioned by General Don as a memorial to General Sir Augustus Eliott who led the British force that took the Rock in 1704. The original statue was carved from the bowsprit of a Spanish vessel taken at the Battle of Trafalgar. The statue was taken to the Convent in 1858 and replaced by the bronze bust of General Eliot that stands there today. There are three 10-inch and one 8-inch howitzer surrounding the statue, all dating from the late 18th century.

*From the Eliott Memorial, follow the nearby steps upward to the area of the Garden known as **the Dell**.*

This garden was laid out by a Genoese gardener in 1842 but the two fountains and large Castle and Key insignia were added at a later date. Access to the lower part of the Dell is restricted but is best enjoyed from the bridge in any event.

Passing the Dell and the distinctive whalebone gate on its southern side, continue past the Molly Bloom statue until you arrive at the **Wellington Memorial***, which was also erected by Sir George Don.*

The memorial to the popular Duke of Wellington was funded by deducting a day's pay from each member of the Garrison. Wellington's bronze bust sits on a marble pillar brought to Gibraltar from the Roman ruins of Lepida in present-day Libya. The memorial is flanked on either side by 13-inch mortars with shells, and has a bronze 12-pound gun on a wooden carriage dating back to the mid 18th century at its front.

The Alameda Gardens
Red Sands Road
PO Box 843
Gibraltar
Tel. +350 200 41235
Fax + 350 200 74022
E-mail info@gibraltargardens.gi
Open: 8am-9pm or until sunset if earlier.
Prices: Gardens: free; Wildlife Park: £2 (adults) and £1.50 (children)

Follow the steps down from the Wellington Memorial and exit the gardens onto Red Sands Road, which descends onto Rosia Road. You should continue to walk south past the **South Jumper's Bastion** *keeping the adjacent dock-yard on your right hand side.*

If you are feeling peckish, Jumper's Wheel Restaurant on the nearby North Jumper's Bastion is a favourite with the locals and offers a comprehensive menu comprising many traditional meat and fresh seafood dishes.

Follow the road past the BP petrol station as it gradually inclines and snakes off to the left, passing the dockyard's clock tower on your right hand side and New Mole House Police Station on your left.

You may want to drop in on the **100-ton gun** situated on Napier of Magdala Battery and should certainly not avoid the area known as Nelson's Anchorage where HMS Victory was towed after the Battle of Trafalgar with Nelson's body on board famously preserved in a casket of rum (the 100-ton gun and Nelson's Anchorage are described in more detail in Walks 5 and 4 respectively).

100-Ton Gun
Napier of Magdala Battery
Rosia Road
Gibraltar
Tel. +350 200 40280
E-mail tourism@gibraltar.gi
Open: Daily, 9.30am-7pm
Price: £1

Continue as best you can along the edge of the line wall until you reach the series of batteries known as **Parsons Lodge**.

This fascinating complex of underground tunnels and gun emplacements was originally developed during the Moorish occupation of the Rock and visitors are treated to some unique views across the Bay and Strait. Although this site tends to get overlooked by many visitors it is a must-see for military enthusiasts. Unfortunately at the the time of writing, Parson's Lodge Battery is closed to the general public in order to undergo a series of refurbishments. For more up-to-date information on the Battery contact the Gibraltar Tourist Board on +350 200 74950 or email information@tourism.gov.gi.

After exploring Parsons Lodge, make your way through the nearby tunnel to the area known as Camp Bay.

This is a large recreation and leisure area that is extremely popular during Gibraltar's official bathing season, which roughly spans from June to September. Follow the length of the promenade and you will see on the Rock face on your left hand side a manmade waterfall that is actually the outfall from one of Gibraltar's desalination plants. At the end of Camp Bay, a path alongside the Nuffield Pool leads to Little Bay but you should follow the hill upwards passing through the Keightley Way tunnel which connects Camp Bay with the area known as Europa Flats. Like so many other sites in Gibraltar, the tunnel is named after one of its former governors, in this case General Sir Charles Keightley who was governor of Gibraltar from 1958 to 1962. This was the last surface tunnel to be cut in Gibraltar, incorporating a practical pedestrian lane on its right hand side, which you are advised to stay within as you navigate your way through to Europa.

The first thing you will see after negotiating the tunnel is the **Ibrahim-al-Ibrahim Mosque**. The Mosque of the Two Holy Mosques was a gift from King Fahad Al-Saud of Saudi Arabia and was officially opened by the King himself in the summer of 1997. The spectacular white dome and turret were built at a cost of about £5 million and the complex also contains a school, a library and a lecture hall. The construction took just two years to complete. The location of the Mosque was said to be an important consideration for King Fahad, since its proximity to Gibraltar's southernmost point allows worshippers (many of whom are Moroccan) views of their homeland across the Strait of Gibraltar. A guided tour of the Mosque can be arranged free of charge but the rules of the Mosque must naturally be respected, including the wearing of modest clothing for both men and women. Females may not be able to enter all areas of the Mosque and will need to wear an ankle-length skirt or trousers, a long-sleeved and high-necked top and may be asked to wear a headscarf.

Ibrahim-al-Ibrahim Mosque.

Europa Point
PO Box 615
Gibraltar
To arrange a guided tour of the Mosque, telephone +350 200 77770

In front of the Mosque and in a largely dilapidated state is an underground cistern known locally as **Nun's Well**. This naturally occurring well probably got its name from the nuns of the **Shrine of Our Lady of Europa**, who were

said to bathe nearby. The Shrine itself is east of Nun's Well and is well worth a visit being one of several churches on the Rock that were converted from mosques when Muslim Gibraltar was captured by the Christian Monarchs. A fragment of pavement outside the Shrine was said to have dated back to the Middle Ages, but is more likely to have been laid down at the beginning of the 18th century. The building was also used as a guard room by the British and an old whipping post dating back to that time can still be seen outside the Shrine. Years before the nearby lighthouse was built, a light shining in the tower acted as a warning signal for sailors passing through the Straits. A special mass is celebrated in the Shrine once a year on Europe Day (May 5) and in 2009, a special ceremony was held to celebrate 700 years of devotion to our Lady of Europe, which began when King Ferdinand IV of Spain overcame the Muslim enclave in Gibraltar. Gibraltar was recovered by the Merinids just 24 years later in 1333 and Gibraltar remained under Muslim rule until 1462. After having been thrown into the sea by British marines in 1704, the original wooden statue of Our Lady of Europe, which can still be seen in the Shrine, was found by a fisherman and kept in Algeciras until it was returned to Gibraltar in 1864.

Shrine of Our Lady of Europe
Europa Point
Gibraltar
Tel. +350 200 71230 and +350 200 77138
Fax +350 20073962
E-mail rector@ourladyofeurope.net
www.ourladyofeurope.net
Open: Monday-Friday, 10.30am-6.30pm (closed Wednesdays);
Saturday, 11am-6pm (Holy Mass held at 12pm)

One of the most prominent features of the area is **The Lighthouse**, which is the most southerly of all Trinity lighthouses (being the only one outside the

United Kingdom). It has been in operation since 1841 and became fully automated in 1994 at which time the Lighthouse Keeper's residence was converted into private homes.

*The Lighthouse marks **Europa Point** and therefore the end of your walk from the northern to southernmost tip of Gibraltar.*

On a clear day, Europa Point is also undoubtedly one of the best places to enjoy the spectacular views across the Strait of Gibraltar towards Africa and most prominently, the mountain known as Jabal Musa. Left of Jabal Musa you can see, just 14.5mi away on the African mainland, the Spanish autonomous city of Ceuta overlooked by Monte Hacho, a low mountain considered the southern mythical pillar of Hercules. You can follow the Moroccan coastline eastwards until it disappears behind the Spanish mainland at Punta Carnero, 5mi from the Rock.

The number 3 bus can be taken back to town or the border from Europa Point or indeed via the alternative walking route described below.

The Dudley Ward Tunnel (named after Sir Alfred Dudley Ward, Governor of Gibraltar, 1962 to 1965) links Europa with the Eastern part of the Rock and was reopened in 2011 after having been closed for nine years. If you follow the steep incline south of the roundabout which lies adjacent to the Mosque, you will reach the tunnel itself. From here, the route will take you in the direction of the frontier along a more direct route along Devil's Tower Road, passing Sandy Bay, Catalan Bay and Eastern Beach in the process. This walk however continues north from said roundabout onto Europa Road which follows a gentle gradient past various colonial-style properties towards the Naval Hospital.

This hospital was built in 1744 at this location to shelter it from the Spanish land batteries and to minimize the effect of the humid levanter conditions that affect the Rock. A little further on, the area known as the Mount, now an exclusive residential district, was the residence of Gibraltar's Senior Naval Officer since it was purchased from General Sir William Green in 1799 for the sum of £1,500.

At its highest point, Europa Road passes by the **Loreto Convent** – a private school originally run by Loretto nuns, an order that comprised members of the Institute of the Blessed Virgin Mary – before continuing north past the iconic Rock Hotel. Arguably Gibraltar's most famous hotel, its guests down the years have included Winston Churchill and Hollywood A-listers such as Rita Heyworth, Errol Flynn and Sean Connery. In May of 1935, after the fall of Addis Ababa, Emperor Haile Selassie spent a night in this hotel en route to England.

Continue to descend towards the town area and Main Street where you can follow the reverse route back to the frontier.

– Walk 4 –
Naval Gibraltar

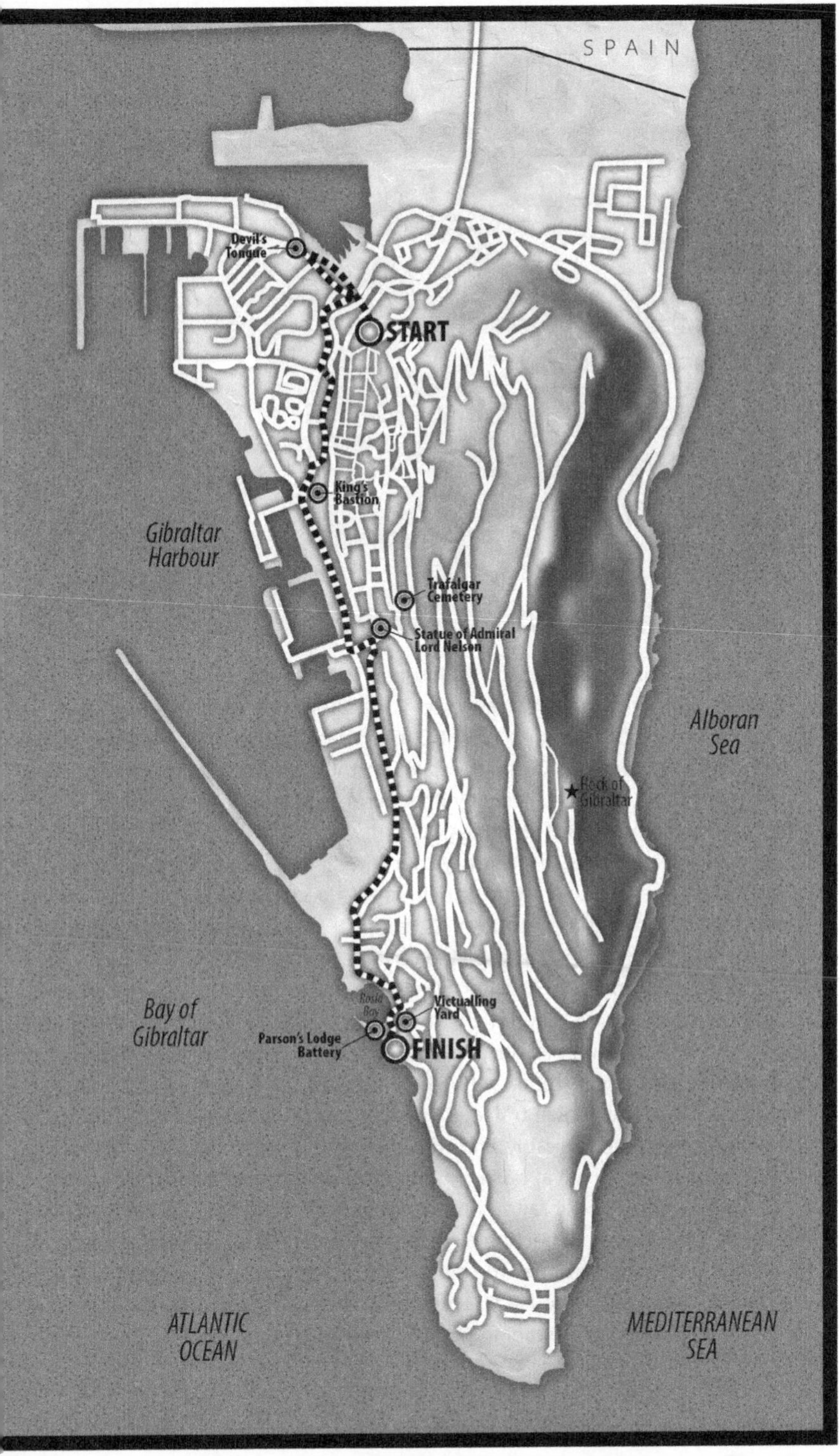

SPAIN

Devil's Tongue

START

King's Bastion

Gibraltar Harbour

Trafalgar Cemetery

Statue of Admiral Lord Nelson

Alboran Sea

Rock of Gibraltar

Bay of Gibraltar

Rosia Bay

Victualling Yard

Parson's Lodge Battery

FINISH

ATLANTIC OCEAN

MEDITERRANEAN SEA

The Strait of Gibraltar has been an intrinsic part of Mediterranean trade routes since Phoenician seafarers traversed it on their way to trading outposts in Western Europe from around 1500 BC. Gibraltar was sacred to the Phoenicians and artefacts founds at Gorham's Cave on the eastern coast of the Rock are testament to its use as a shrine by Phoenician and later Carthaginian mariners between the 8th and 3rd centuries BC.

It was not until the 17th century that British trade with the Mediterranean was properly established and British sailors began to acquaint themselves with the area round the Strait of Gibraltar. It soon became apparent to the British that a naval base in the Mediterranean was necessary to further the interests of its Empire; Gibraltar was soon touted as a possible location. In 1655 Oliver Cromwell noted the twin benefits of Gibraltar as: "an advantage to our trade and an annoyance to the Spaniards" with whom Britain was at war at the time. More importantly Gibraltar's advantage lay in its commanding position at the centre of Mediterranean trade routes and the fact that it could be maintained cheaply and with a relatively small garrison. The development of a British naval base in Tangiers and the better facilities available at Cadiz meant that Gibraltar's time was not to come for another 49 years, however in 1704, as a reaction to the changing political situation in the area, an Anglo-Dutch force under the command of Admiral Sir George Rooke took the Rock. The key to the Mediterranean was now in British hands and it has remained an important staging point for the Royal Navy to this day.

Getting your bearings: This walk begins at the northern end of Casemates Square at the site of the medieval galley house and follows a route outside the old city walls up to the Trafalgar Cemetery on the southern end of Main Street before visiting Gibraltar's dockyard, the area known as Nelson's Anchorage and the series of coastal batteries known as Parson's Lodge.

Length: Approximately 2.5km/1.5mi (2 hours)

Gibraltar's medieval harbour was located approximately where Casemates Square now stands. Although protected from easterly and westerly winds, this harbour remained at the mercy of the fierce south-westerly winds that affect the Bay and was therefore built within the city's walls and accessed via a small inlet which run through the Water Gate into the location of the present square. The original Water Gate was positioned just north of the present **Grand Casemates Gate** and the bricked-up arch of this gate was discernable until the line wall was reconstructed in 18th Century. The remains of the structure still visible at Casemates Square, in a fenced enclosure outside of the Little Rock bar is the southern wall of the medieval atarazana or galleyhouse, a roofed jetty about 40m in length where the medieval inhabitants of the town would have repaired their galleys or protected them during enemy attack or stormy weather. The Galley House was altered and used for alternative means before eventually being used as a shot house during the early years of British occupation. Like many of the buildings in the north of the town, the Galley House was damaged during the Great Siege and was prob-

ably destroyed completely towards the end of the 18th century when the Casemates Barracks were being built. Although part of the atarazana's foundations were excavated during the Square's recent renovation, the rest remain concealed below the Barracks.

*Make your way out of Grand Casemates Gate, passing the Public Market on your left and through the curtain wall towards the Waterport Roundabout. You should continue walking west onto the area once known as the **Devil's Tongue**, now Waterport Wharf Road, which is flanked by residential property on both sides.*

The Devil's Tongue, known as such by the Spanish due to the damage it was said to have inflicted on Spanish shipping in the Bay, was originally built as an extension of the Old, Mole which itself had been rebuilt and extended many times since it was first constructed in a primitive form during the Merinid occupation. The mole originally extended from Chatham's Counterguard and a drawbridge known as the Chatham Wicket led from within the city walls to the mole. The original opening in the sea wall, now bricked-up, is still visible on Chatham Counterguard.

The Devil's Tongue in its present form was built during the Great Siege and constructed with the intention of bringing flanking fire on the Spanish lines. However on recommendation from General Sir John Burgoyne, inspector-general of fortifications who visited the Rock in 1848, the defences of the Devil's Tongue were turned around to provide south-facing protection to the harbour rather than be pointed towards the isthmus where they had proved to be highly ineffective. It now has an extension on its western flank about 487m long running in the direction of the Detached Mole as well as five additional jetties. These jetties were built during the early part of the last century as a commercial mole but were soon taken over by the Admiralty to ac-

commodate destroyer flotillas, only being returned to the civilian authorities in the 1960s. Land reclamation on either side of the mole and the mole extension make it hard to imagine how the Devil's Tongue would have looked during its early life.

Also on Waterport Wharf Road is a statue of Admiral Sir George Rooke, the first British military governor of Gibraltar having commanded the allied naval forces during the capture of the Rock on July 21, 1704. The statue was erected in 2004 to commemorate the tercentenary of this event.

Retracing your footsteps back to the Waterport roundabout, turn right and make your way along the outside of the Montagu Counterguard onto Queens-way, formerly known as Reclamation Road but renamed after Queen Elizabeth II when she visited Gibraltar in 1954 as part of her Commonwealth Tour.

It should be remembered that a large portion of the land situated outside of the counterguard has been reclaimed from the sea in the last 20 years. The **Montagu Pavilion**, on your right hand side as you follow the curve of the road, was, as recently as the late 1980s, a bathing pavilion on the sea front, only later converted into modern offices.

Continue along the exterior edge of the line wall for about 500m past the American War Memorial and Prince Albert's Front until you reach Kings Bastion. Before reaching the Bastion, you should follow the steps up to Line Wall Promenade where you can get a good view of **HMS Rooke**, the main naval base in Gibraltar. HMS Rooke is one of the last remaining dedicated Royal Navy shore establishments outside of the UK and was established in June 1946 on land reclaimed during World War II. Although the Royal Navy's presence in the Mediterranean has virtually disappeared, Gibraltar still remains the main British naval base outside of the UK and, under the Commander British Forces Gibraltar, is home to the Gibraltar Squadron. This is a fully operational front-line squadron consisting of two 16-m Patrol Launches and 3 Arctic 6.5-m Rigid Inflatable Boats manned by a team of 19 personnel whose aim is to safeguard the security and integrity of British Gibraltar Territorial Waters.

Before returning to Queensway, you will note the rear of the building, which is now Gibraltar's City Hall and was built by wealthy Gibraltarian merchant Aaron Cardozo. Cardozo was an entrepreneur with many business interests, inlcluding the supply of beef to the Navy. He was also a personal friend of Admiral Nelson and the Admiral was known to have visited Cardozo in Gibraltar in June 1805, just months before the Battle of Trafalgar. Gibraltar was in a terrible state at the time and was still recovering from the recent yellow fever epidemic that had killed half the civilian population, and Nelson is said to have whispered: "If I survive Cardozo you shall no longer remain in this dark corner of the world." A few months later when Nelson's fleet was blockading Cadiz and were in short supply of beef, Nelson sent Cardozo on the HMS Termagant to broker a deal with the Bey of Oran. When personal mementoes were being distributed among Nelson's friends and colleagues after his death in October 1805, Cardozo was sent a gold medal commemorating another of Nelson's great victories in the Battle of the Nile.

*Returning onto Queensway you will notice, adjacent to the Naval Base at No.4 Dock, the home of the **Gibraltar Sea Scouts**.*

The Gibraltar Sea Scouts, formed in 1915 with Mr Ratcliffe RN, as their first Scoutmaster paraded in uniform for the first time in Gibraltar on Empire Day of that year. They are the only Sea Scout group outside the UK that are recognized by the Admiralty. The Sea Scouts originally worked as messengers at the naval, military and civil works and contributed to the war effort when they loaned their boat the Eider Duck, to the Royal Navy who used it as a tender for the duration of World War II.

This area is also the home of the **Royal Gibraltar Yacht Club** (RGYC), which was relocated fully to nearby Coaling Island in 2012 and is one of the oldest yacht clubs in the world having been founded in 1829 by officers of various regiments stationed on the Rock. The Gibraltar Chronicle of July 15, 1829 gave notice of a meeting of the Gibraltar Yacht Club that was to be held at the Griffiths Hotel where a plea was made for any interested parties to attend. The RGYC operates in much the same way as it has done throughout its history, although it is perhaps a little less active than it was when Gibraltar's naval base was fully operational. While the Club's culture is more democratic these days, membership still conveys a certain element of social status in Gibraltar, however ownership of a yacht is still not an essential prerequisite for membership!

As you continue along Queensway you will pass the Queensway Quay development and before that a small berthing marina, built on the site of the old Coaling Island. The Coaling Island was constructed around the turn of the last century in conjunction with the other Dockyard works.

Prior to the building of the Queensway Quay residential and commercial development, most Royal Navy ships that docked in Gibraltar would do so in this area. It must have been an impressive sight to observe the Royal Navy's Gibraltar-based fleet, which protected the entrance to the Mediterranean (known as Force H) anchored near here during World War II. A residential development known as Cormorant Wharf has been named in honour of **HMS Cormorant**, a composite sloop which was originally an accommodation ship that came to Gibraltar in 1889 serving in the defence of the Rock for 60 years,

of which 37 years were spent moored in this area. Originally her armament consisted of two 6-inch and six 5-inch Muzzleloader cannons, but after being re-commissioned as Gibraltar's Depot Ship she was reduced to a saluting battery of just four 3-pounders. She mounted automatic 20mm anti-aircraft guns during World War II and was eventually broken up in Malaga in 1949. Another famous incident that occurred in this area was the explosion onboard the Naval Armament Carrier RFA Bedenham on April 27, 1951. While tied up at the nearby Gun Wharf, the ship caught fire and blew up killing 13 people and causing extensive damage to the town area.

A small roundabout adorned with a large anchor lies at the end of Queensway, opposite the Navy Boat Sheds, marking the entrance to the **Dockyard***.*

It was near here that the Dockyard's impressive North Gate had stood until it was controversially demolished overnight and without public consultation in the early 1990s in an attempt to widen the road. The Dockyard was built in its present form around the turn of the 20th century under contract by British engineering firm Topham, Jones and Railton, who also built the South Mole, the commercial mole extension to the North Mole and the Detached Mole. Prior to these improvements, which began in 1895, Gibraltar still lacked a secure anchorage and dockyard facilities capable of dealing with the increasing requirements of the Royal Navy. There was a small careening bay and various boat sheds as well as a small mole, however plans to move the Channel Squadron to Gibraltar meant that vast improvements needed to be made to Gibraltar's port facilities to accommodate their needs.

France remained Britain's main naval rival and Gibraltar's importance lay in its guardianship over the narrow Strait that divided France's two main naval bases; Brest in the Atlantic and Toulon in the Mediterranean. A multi-million pound project commenced and thousands of labourers were recruited from all over Andalusia. In all, an area of 448 acres was enclosed by the moles, 64 acres of which was reclaimed from the sea to accommodate the Dockyard itself. Most of the buildings in the Dockyard, including the **Admiralty Tower** were built around this time. These included a gun wharf, stores and offices as well as a railway, which run along Queensway to the North Mole. In addition a 321-m tunnel was excavated beneath the Rock connecting the dockyard to the quarries on the eastern side of the Rock. A better view of the Dockyard can be enjoyed from the Saluting Battery, which will be visited later on this walk. The base is considerably smaller than it once was, with many of the workshops now being used by private enterprise. Nevertheless the Tower, together with the adjacent wharf and part of the South Mole, is still in use by the Admiralty.

*Walk through **Ragged Staff Gate** and ascend the hill on the left hand side*

of the road.

The name Ragged Staff is a throwback to the early days of British rule when drinking water for the supply of ships was obtained from the Red Sands area. Barrels were taken down what is now Ragged Staff Road to a small wharf where they were loaded onto ships. The loading was facilitated by a small boat with a short mast that acted like a crane mechanism. This type of mast was known to seamen as a ragged staff mast and this name was given to the loading wharf and later to the gate and adjoining road.

As you follow Ragged Staff Road, you will see a car parking area on your left hand side. In 2012, a series of buildings and workshops once occupied by the Buildings and Works Department, known as the 'Patio Chico' were cleared to expose this open area together with a late Nineteenth Century ammunition magazine. The Victorian magazine, at the western end of the parking area, originally housed the ammunition for the 10-inch, 18-ton RML guns which were located atop South Bastion, before beging decommissioned for use as a pumphouse at the turn of the last century.

Turn left at the top of Ragged Staff Road, following the line of the Spanish-built South Bastion.

In front of South Bastion's high eastern wall is a **Statue of Admiral Lord Nelson**, erected in 2005 to commemorate 200 years since the Battle of Trafalgar. Nelson, as already mentioned, features prominently in the history of Gibraltar, a place he affectionately termed "the good old Rock". He often wrote about the importance of Gibraltar both as a base for the supply of the Royal Navy fleet and for its prominent position at the entrance to the Mediterranean. Many famous sea battles have taken place near Gibraltar including the Battle of Cape St Vincent where Nelson distinguished himself as a young Commodore and the Battle of Trafalgar where the Admiral lost his life aged only 47 years.

Opposite Nelson's statue and within Southport Ditch (part of the Rock's defences dating back to the Spanish occupation) is the **Trafalgar Cemetery**. The cemetery was in fact originally known as Southport Ditch Cemetery and was consecrated for use in 1798. Most of the graves do not belong to people who died during the Battle of Trafalgar and the cemetery only took its present name many years later. A plaque on the cemetery's southern wall references other nearby naval battles of the period such as Algeciras (1801),

Cádiz (1810) and Málaga (1812) and the remains of servicemen who fell during these conflicts are also interred in the Cemetery. The majority of the graves however, belong to servicemen and their families who died during one of several epidemics that blighted Gibraltar around the turn of the 19th century. Graves numbered 121 and 101 are the only ones that contain the remains of servicemen who were wounded during the Battle of Trafalgar and who later died at the Naval Hospital in Gibraltar. Captain Thomas Norman was a Royal Marine serving on the HMS Mars and Lieutenant William Forster was only 20 years of age when he perished serving on board HMS Colossus. The majority of those who perished at the Battle of Trafalgar were buried at sea. An anchor monument can be seen at the southern end of the cemetery. This was donated by the Royal Navy in 1992 and an inscription quotes Admiral Collingwood's despatch reporting victory at the Battle of Trafalgar and Nelson's death.

Make your way past the Trafalgar Sports Bar up to the Piccadilly Bar, located on the northern end of the Saluting Battery known locally as la bateria The Saluting Battery, positioned atop the line wall is protected by the North

and South Jumper's Bastions and you should follow the length of the line wall parallel to the dockyard's southern extreme near the three dry docks.

The first dock to be built in Gibraltar was the 140-m No.3 Dock named King Edward VII's Dock as King Edward had set its coping stone during a visit to Gibraltar in 1903. It was completed in 1905. The No.2 Dock, known as Alexandra Dock, was 168m long and named after Queen Alexandra who inaugurated it in 1904. The largest of the docks, the No.1 Dock, has an overall length of 259m and was built as a double dock that could hold two ships at one time, divided by a steel caisson. This dock was named after the then Prince and Princess of Wales (later to become George V and Queen Mary) who visited the Rock on their way back from a visit to India in 1906

The **South Mole** (formerly known as the New Mole) extends from the location of the present dry docks for a total of 1,085m into the Bay of Gibraltar. Construction of the original mole began in the early 17th century under the supervision of Philip IV of Spain and its landward side was defended by a defensive fortification called the Torre del Tuerto (Tower of the One-eyed Man). Progress was slow and after ten years of construction, the mole was only 24 feet long. The matter began to advance again in 1626 under the governorship of Luis Bravo de Acuña, however it was not until 1670 that the Mole had reached the respectable length of 329m and the tower located at its head was replaced by a modern gun battery. The British extended the South Mole to its present length using contractors Topham, Jones and Railton and 700,000 tons of quarried rock, which was floated into position in barges. It was also at this time that the **Detached Mole** was constructed using sloping blocks of concrete weighing between 18 and 36 tons a piece, which were lowered into position by two large Titan cranes. The last block was set on the northern side of the Detached Mole by King George V, the then Duke of York.

The area adjacent to where the dockyard's clock tower now stands once had the dubious honour of having been home to a HM prison establishment. When the transportation of convicts to Australia stopped in 1837, the British Government had to consider alternative arrangements and in 1841 a penal settlement with 200 convicts was set up in Gibraltar on board an old navy frigate HMS Owen Glendower. Convict numbers increased dramatically in the ensuing years reaching a peak of almost 900 convicts in 1849 and prisoners were moved to purpose-built cells set against the line wall. Much of the work on the Moles during this period (including the lengthening of the New Mole to 427m) was carried out by convict labour, however it was soon established that imported labour from Spain would be far less expensive and in 1875 the final prisoners were shipped back to Britain and the penal establishment terminated. Subsequent work on the Dockyard was carried out by Spanish labourers and at its peak almost 5,000 Spaniards crossed the border into Gibraltar daily to get their hands on the relatively high daily wage of 2 shillings and 3 pence offered by HM government.

Carry on walking south with the coast on your right hand side, following Rosia Road as it slowly ascends before arching down to the left.

The word *Rosia* supposedly comes from a monastery town in Tuscany of the same name and pre-dates the British occupation of Gibraltar. There are numerous grand colonial-style properties in the area, many of which would have originally belonged to high-ranking naval officers but are now mainly privately owned residences. Many of the modern developments in the area reflect Gibraltar's naval heritage, including The Anchorage, Admiral's Place and Nelson's View as well as the nearby headquarters of the Royal Gibraltar Police at New Mole House.

Napier of Magdala Battery is home to the 100-ton gun and offers excellent views of Rosia Bay, a small cove that holds the distinction of being Gibraltar's only natural anchorage. Several embrasures in the line wall adjacent to the Rosia Plaza building also offer an excellent vantage of the bay. The small wharf, which is still in place today, was added in 1812 before the building of the New Mole (South Mole) shifted the naval concentration on the Rock further north. The area is perhaps most famous for being the bay into which a damaged HMS Victory was towed by HMS Neptune on October 28, 1805 with Nelson's body on board, preserved in a barrel of spirits. The Victory remained anchored in Rosia Bay for six days while her masts and rigging were repaired before setting sail on the month-long journey to England, flying Nelson's flag at half-mast. Nelson was granted a state funeral, something which at the time was totally unprecedented for a person who was not of royal blood. An elaborate affair saw his body taken in a ship-shaped funeral carriage to St Paul's Cathedral where he was buried in an Italian marble sarcophagus that can still be seen there today.

Walk around the edge of the Rosia Plaza building in the direction of Rosia Bay.

You soon arrive in the area of the Victualling Yard and adjacent water tanks, which were built at the behest of Admiral of the Fleet Sir John Jervis who was created Earl St Vincent for his famous naval victory at the Battle of St Vincent on St Valentine's Day, 1797. St Vincent had come ashore at Gibraltar after this great victory, finding himself modest quarters at Rosia House, and set out to reorganize the dockyard facilities in Gibraltar in the area of the old Rosia swimming club, which was at the time Gibraltar's only harbour. The Navy stores and water reserves had previously been located in the Casemates area in order to service ships anchored on the Old Mole. As the range of enemy artillery fire increased, it made sense to move the Naval Base to the southern end of the peninsular and as far away from Spanish cannon fire as possible.

Four cottages known as Rosia Cottages and originally built for victualling personnel in the 19th century mark the western extreme of where the original water reservoir known later as the Rosia Tanks were situated. These were completed in 1804 and were built to purify and store up to 6 million litres of water for the provision of Royal Navy fleets visiting Gibraltar via a complex gravity feed system that reached the harbour below the location of the present road. Some remnants of the feed system can still be viewed on the steep access ramp leading down to Rosia Bay. The tanks were almost 10m deep and over a million bricks were needed to build it. These bricks were shipped over from Britain and the structure, completed with a sand-lime mortar, was still in use by the MOD as recently as the 1970s. The tanks were constructed with sloping vaulted roofs designed to catch water. Despite a campaign to save the Rosia Tanks, they were sadly destroyed in 2007 to make way for modern apartments.

The adjacent **Victualling Yard** however, still remains, and this was completed at a total cost of £60,000 in 1812 to store dry provisions. It is a quite enormous building, measuring some 58m x 49m over two floors and made up of eleven vaulted rooms with impressive arched tunnels on the ground floor and bombproof stone walls. The Yard was designed by local builder Giovanni Maria Boschetti and he was responsible for the inscription above the door which reads "G.III D G M B & H R & c." or "Georgius III Deo Gratia Maiestate Britanniae et Hibernias Rex & c." (George III, Monarch of Great Britain and King of Ireland, etc.). It is perhaps no coincidence that his initials GMB appear within this inscription. Like the Tanks, the Victualling Yard's roofs were designed with a sloping surface to collect rain water, which would then be stored in the adjacent tanks.

This walk concludes at the adjacent **Parsons Lodge Battery**. This area actually comprises a series of batteries that stand 30m above Rosia Bay on a shelf of limestone rock and tend to get overlooked by many visitors to Gibraltar. Whilst Parson's Lodge would usually be a must-see attraction for those with anything more than a passing interest in Gibraltar's history, particularly military enthusiasts, it is unfortunately closed to the public currently. Due to its prominent position, the site had originally been developed during the Muslim occupation of the Rock and later by the Spanish. The fortifications were improved by the British who felt it necessary to protect Rosia Bay and sentries on duty. Sentries on duty in Parson's Lodge would have witnessed the HMS Victory being towed into Rosia Bay in October 1805 after the Battle of Trafalgar.

There are a multitude of 6-pounder gun emplacements with some cannon still in their original positions. In 1872 the battery was adjusted to accommodate three 18-ton, 10-inch RMLs that were positioned behind so-called Gibraltar Shields made of iron and teak. The remains of the expense magazines as well as various shell hoists and stores gives the visitor a good indication of what some of the batteries must have been like before they were decommissioned in 1956. In the years immediately prior to decommissioning, Parson's Lodge had been mainly used as a coastal searchlight position and benefitted from its own generating station. Visitors are provided with a plan of the complex, which is made up of a series of underground tunnels and gun emplacements offering spectacular views across the Bay and Strait. There is a small visitor's centre and plenty of information available on site about Parson's Lodge and its significance to the Rock. It is interesting to note that the name Parson's Lodge seems to be a loose reference to the hermitage of St John the Green, which was situated in close proximity to the batteries.

For more up-to-date information on the Battery contact the Gibraltar Tourist Board on +350 200 74950 or email information@tourism.gov.gi

– Walk 5 –
Guns of Gibraltar

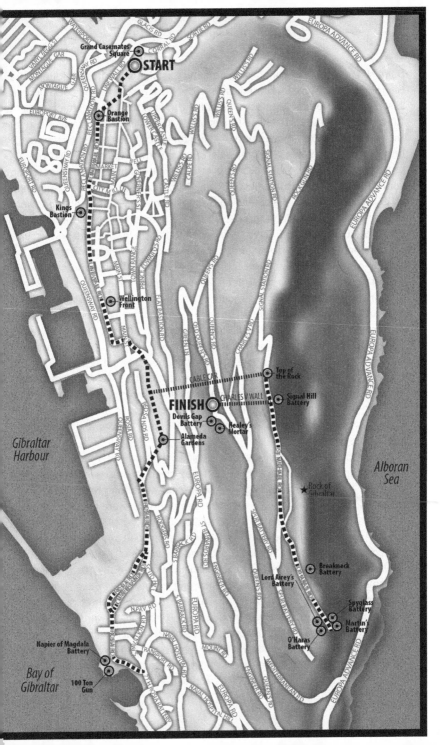

Spanish Muslims used cannons against the Castilian army in 1342 during the Siege of Algeciras, just a few miles from the Rock across the Bay of Gibraltar. Just 7 years later cannons were used for the first time in an attack against Gibraltar, this time by Castilian forces under King Alfonso XI. It was not until the late 15th century, however, that Gibraltar officially deployed heavy weaponry of its own. When Gibraltar was captured from Spain in 1704, the attacking commanders found Gibraltar to be a well-fortified fortress mounting some 400 guns. Unfortunately for Spain, Gibraltar was not as well garrisoned as it was fortified and the defending troops, numbering some 150 men, were unprepared for the sudden surprise attack. In a matter of hours Gibraltar had capitulated and after being formerly ceded to Britain in 1713, its new occupiers were intent on not making the same mistakes as their predecessors.

Early reports of British ordnance on the Rock state that in the early years of British rule Gibraltar was defended by nothing more than six 13-inch mortars and twenty-four guns mounted on ships' carriages, suggesting that most of the guns inherited from the Spanish must have been either damaged or become obsolete. By 1726 during the second siege of British Gibraltar, the British garrison was said to have had about 70 guns and mortars protecting it, although most of these were damaged beyond repair during the Siege. By 1744 Gibraltar had built its armament up to 339 guns. Though this appeared to be a respectable amount and was complemented by a garrison of some 3,000 troops, they were a mismatch of brass and iron cannon of various types and calibre making the acquisition of spares and ammunition a constant problem.

It was not until the tenure of chief engineer William Green during the mid-18th century that Gibraltar's armament was given a comprehensive overhaul including the standardization of weaponry and numerous renovations of its defensive fortifications. By the mid-19th century there were 680 guns ranging from iron-cast 6 to 32-pounders mounted on 110 batteries. In 1870 two enormous 100-ton guns arrived at the Rock and the one on Lord Napier of Magdala Battery still remains. As artillery continued to develop, rifled muzzle-loading guns (RMLs) were replaced by Breach-loading guns (BLs). By 1914, Gibraltar's armament consisted of thirteen 9.2-inch and twenty 6-inch BLs as well as a range of Quick Firing guns that protected the harbour at short range. World War II heralded a move away from siege fortifications towards anti-aircraft guns and coastline defence weaponry. At its peak, twenty-eight 3.7-inch guns, forty-eight 40mm Bofors and various QF 2-pounder Mk II & VIII guns protected the Rock and remnants of these and many other of the above mentioned guns can still be seen on the bastions and batteries around Gibraltar.

Getting your bearings: This walk covers a selection of Gibraltar's guns, starting in the town area and walking via Kings Bastion and the Alameda Gardens up to Gibraltar's famous 100-ton gun. You will then take the cable car to the top of the Rock to enjoy the spectacular views from the 9.2-inch batteries at the upper ridge of the Rock before visiting Healey's Mortar and Devil's Gap Battery on your way back into town. Note that an adult's single ticket to the top of the Rock by cable car costs £8 (£9.75 return) and £4 (£4.50 return) for children. The last cable car departs from the Grand Parade daily at 5.15pm and at 7.15pm during the summer season.

Length: Approximately 4km /2.5mi (4.5 hours)

This walk begins at Grand Casemates Square, at the northern end of Main Street.

Originally part of the medieval dockyard, this area developed into a residential area lined with houses that enjoyed the protection of the city's walls and the reassuring presence of the Tower of Homage high above it. It has been used as a parade ground and famously played host to Gibraltar's last public hanging in 1864. It is fitting that a walk covering the guns of Gibraltar should begin here, at the town's northern end, due to its proximity to the parallel **Grand Battery**, arguably one of Gibraltar's most impressive defensive fortifications. Currently obscured behind Grand Casemates Barracks, Grand Battery protected the landward approach to Gibraltar via the isthmus and, together with the adjacent North Bastion, mounted no fewer than thirty 24-pounder cannons in 1859. A better view of the Battery, which no longer mounts any cannon, can be enjoyed from Landport Ditch outside the city's walls.

On the western end of Casemates Square another type of gun is given prominence. Positioned on a plinth in front of the Tourist Office, is a replica of the so-called **Koehler Gun** incorporating a design developed in Gibraltar during the Great Siege (1779-1783). The gun is distinctive for its downwards facing barrel, which allowed it to be placed on an embrasure or rocky promontory with a steep angle of depression and be pointed directly at the besieging enemy. The design of this gun has been attributed to Lieutenant George Koehler who served in Gibraltar during the Great Siege. It was first tested in 1782 and was based on a normal wooden garrison carriage split horizontally down its centre with a hinge at the front to adjust the trajectory. Unlike other contemporary guns, the barrel was attached to a sliding timber plank that dealt with the recoil.

Walk in the direction of Main Street and take the first right turning beyond the International Commercial Centre onto Cooperage Lane until you reach

*an archway that marks the northern end of Irish Town. On your left hand side before you reach the archway, a narrow flight of steps takes you onto the line wall between Montagu Bastion to the north (right) and Orange Bastion to the south (left). Cross the road at the nearby zebra crossing and you will soon get an excellent view of the rear of **Orange Bastion**, which excellently illustrates the development of artillery and gun emplacements in Gibraltar during the last two centuries.*

On the left and right flanks, the Bastion's original design can still be appreciated. In 1834 it mounted three 24-pounder, smooth-bore, cast-iron carronades and eight standard 24-pounders. The barrels of various of these cannonades can be seen set into the ground on City Mill Lane where they mark the foot of that hill and on Bomb House Lane near the Gibraltar Museum. The Bastion was upgraded to 32-pounders in 1859 and four of these are still in position on the left and right flanks. These 32-pounders were constructed by the Carron Company, an ironworks based in Falkirk, Scotland. In 1877 the Bastion was converted into a heavy RML battery by the construction of armoured casemates on the face of the Bastion and the mounting of two 10-inch 18-ton RMLs concealed behind iron shields. RMLs marked a new development in artillery in the mid-19th century, which included the introduction of rifling within the gun's barrel giving the gun greater accuracy and increased penetration. The original iron shields still remain and gun barrels have recently been restored to their original positions within the casemate giving a good indication of what the Bastion would have looked like during Victorian times. You will note the thickness of the gun's cast iron barrel, which has been designed to allow it to withstand varying levels of stress at different parts of the barrel. Since the stress is higher on the lower end of the barrel, the barrel is far thicker at the base. The view over the left flank embrasures show further guns, mainly 24-pounders mounted on the Chatham Counterguard that provided advanced cover for Orange Bastion.

Ascend via the steps adjacent to the American War Memorial onto the line wall and walk south on Prince Albert's front.

In 1859 this area of wall mounted eighteen guns of which six were 68-pounders on wooden traversing carriages. A report into Gibraltar's defences at the time had recommended that all cannons on the seafront be 64-pounders however these guns were six of only ten 64-pounders mounted in Gibraltar at the time. In 1879, in line with the improvements made to the adjacent Orange Bastion, a 12.5-inch, 38-ton RML was added to a platform named Zoca Flank Battery on the southern end of Prince Albert's front, where the Catholic Community Centre now stands. You will notice various short flights of steps along the line wall known as banquettes from which soldiers would fire their muskets, as well as various 18th century buildings including an expense magazine.

Continue south along the line wall beyond the community centre and onto Line Wall Promenade where, flanking the City War Memorial on either side, you can see two Russian 24-pounder guns on their original iron mountings.

These guns were taken as prizes by the British during the Crimean War and were later given as a gift to the people of Gibraltar. Despite being cast at the Alexandrovski factory in Russia in 1826, during the reign of Nicholas I, there is a British link to the design of these guns in that the factory was at the time under the directorship of an Englishman named Alexander Foullon. These two guns, together with two more identical weapons were originally placed on the Grand Parade but were removed when the Parade was converted into a car parking area. These two guns were later moved to this spot and the remaining two were restored to the Alameda in 2002 where they flank George Don Gate.

*Continue to the end of Line Wall Promenade, which is marked with a plaque dedicated to General Sir Robert Boyd. From here ascend onto the upper right flank of **Kings Bastion** via a stone staircase.*

This part of the Bastion remains in materially the same state as it was when it was designed in 1773 by Chief Engineer William Green with the assistance of then governor, General Boyd. During the Bastion's early days the right flank mounted five 32-pounders and five 10-inch howitzers, mirroring the guns on the left south-facing flank. The Bastion remained largely the same until 1859 except that at this time its armament was improved by the addition of two

8-inch smooth-bore guns on either flank. During the Bastion's recent reno-vation, five 32-pounders were restored to the embrasures on the right flank giving a realistic view of what the flank would have looked like in the late 18th century. This embrasured wall originally continued along the front of the Bastion but in 1878, following recommendations by Colonel William Jervois, armoured concrete and masonry casemates were added. The covered area in front of you, which has now been converted into a wine bar (of all things!) mounted a 12.5-inch, 38-ton RML in 1878, one of the last heavy RMLs in service in Gibraltar before the introduction of the 6-inch and 9.2-inch BL guns at the turn of the last century.

Entering the casemate you will immediately see to the rear of the bar area a 10-inch, 18-ton RML pointing out towards the Bay through its protective curved iron shield. There would have been a further 10- inch RML in the adja-cent room. In the third (centre) room the larger 12.5-inch, 38-ton RML boasts a peculiar double gun port. Although the two gun ports meant that the gun was capable of a wider field of fire than the traditional single port, this feature did not catch on at the time due to the inherent inefficiencies of moving such a large gun between the ports. Although the gun's slides and carriages have long since been removed, many original features still remain nearby such as the shell hoists that assisted in lifting ammunition from the courtyard to the upper part of the Bastion. The original shell stores have also been put to good use and now house WC facilities. When the guns were in operation, rope mantles would have hung like curtains around the barrel of the guns, protecting the men working the guns from being injured by shell splinters. Unfortunately the mantles, which were in an advanced state of decay, were removed during the Bastion's recent renovation. Continue along through two further rooms, which would have originally mounted 10-inch RMLs, before exiting to the Bastion's left flank. This flank, like the north-facing right flank also mounts five 32-pounders like it did when the Bastion was first constructed.

Exit the Bastion onto an area of the line wall named Sir Herbert Miles Boule-vard, which provides an excellent vantage point to appreciate the southern flank of Kings Bastion as well as the right flank of **Wellington Front** *at the southern end of the Boulevard. This rear of Wellington Front is best viewed from Lovers Lane, which starts at the end of Sir Herbert Miles Boulevard.*

From here you will be able clearly to see banquettes atop the curtain wall to-gether with an expense magazine and various other auxiliary constructions. The Left and Right Bastions were added in 1845 and in 1863 there were six 68-pounders, four 32-pounders and four 8-inch Smooth Bore guns that defended the flanks. In 1879 following the trend of the day, armoured casemates were added to the Right Bastion in order for it to mount a 12.5-inch, 36-ton RML. The gun is no longer in place but the protective curved shield can still be seen from Queensway at the front of the Bastion.

*Continue along Lovers Lane along the rear of the John Mackintosh and Ince's Hall until you reach the rear of South Bastion. From here follow the line of Charles V Wall until you reach the furthest and smallest of the three gates cut through the wall adjacent to the elaborately painted 18-ton, 10-inch RML cannon mounted on its original carriage (Charles V Wall is covered in more detail in Walk 3: North to South). Traverse the Wall and follow the gently upwards sloping hill along the exterior of the Trafalgar Cemetery until you arrive at the Cemetery's south-east corner. Cross the road and, staying to the left, pass through a small tunnel beneath Europa Road onto a walkway at the eastern end of the Grand Parade, which leads into the **Alameda Gardens**.*

There are two 10-inch RMLs on their carriages on this esplanade pointing in a westerly direction towards the Bay of Gibraltar.

Once in the Alameda Gardens, the path forks off to the right and you should continue along it until you reach the Heathfield Steps. At the base of these steps, at either side of George Don Gate, are the two Russian 24-pounder guns previously mentioned and which match those on Line Wall Boulevard.

Before it was converted into a car park, all four of these Crimean guns used to stand at the eastern end of the Grand Parade near where the two 10-inch RMLs now stand. Follow the Heathfield Steps up to Eliott's Monument, which is surrounded by various 18th-century mortars also known as howitzers. These infantry support weapons differ from ordinary cannons in that they were used to fire shells over short ranges with a high arcing trajectory. Its ability to engage targets outside of the clear line of fire is a mortar's main advantage, although there are also disadvantages such as a loss of accuracy and the inability to use them at very close range. There are three 10-inch and one smaller 8-inch howitzer set into the ground surrounding the statue, all dating from the late 18th century.

*You should continue south through the park until you arrive at **Wellington's Column**, which is flanked by larger 13-inch mortars with their original shells. At the front of the memorial there is a bronze 12-pounder dating from 1758 on a timber garrison carriage.*

*Exit the Gardens onto Red Sands Road and make your way south along the line wall, past the Dockyard to what may possibly be the most impressive, certainly the largest, gun you will encounter on your walk, the **100-ton gun**.*

Situated on **Napier of Magdala Battery**, this gun (which actually weighs 100.2 tons) is one of only twelve guns of its type produced by Sir WG Armstrong Whitworth & Co Ltd, a major manufacturing company based in

Newcastle-Upon-Tyne that was the main British artillery producer at the end of the 19th century. On a barbette Mark I mounting, the gun, which arrived in Gibraltar on December 10, 1882 on board the SS Stanley was one of two guns of this calibre brought to Gibraltar to bolster the Rock's defences. The barrel of the original gun at Napier of Magdala Battery split during a practise firing in 1898 and the second gun, which was mounted on Victoria Battery (on the present site of Gibraltar's Fire Station), was moved to this location as it was thought to command a better position over the Strait. The gun at Napier of Magdala Battery is the best remaining example of only two surviving 100-ton guns anywhere in the world; the other can be seen at Fort Rinella on the island of Malta.

Prior to the construction of the 100-ton gun, the largest gun made by British manufacturers was a 17.72-inch RML, with a mass of 38-tons that shot an 818-pound projectile capable of piercing 16 inches of steel at a distance of 1,829m. Armstrong had offered a prototype of the much larger 100-ton gun to the Royal Navy, however, they rejected its design due to the gun's enormous weight and its projected costs of manufacture. Eight similar guns were then sold to the Italian Navy forcing Britain to order two guns apiece for their important naval bases in Malta and Gibraltar. In its heyday, the 100-ton gun would have been able to propel a 2,000-pound shell to a distance of about 8mi. The gun required about 35 people to operate it but was capable of firing a round that could penetrate 63.5cm of wrought iron, every 4 minutes.

The gun, which had been lying in an almost derelict state since 1906, was renovated and was fired in 2002. During World War II, the battery also mounted four 3.7-inch anti-aircraft guns and one of these is still present on the Battery's flank, just above the 100-ton gun. The barrel of the original Napier of Magdala gun is said to be buried underneath the Fortress Headquarters building adjacent to the battery where it forms part of its foundations. There is an Interpretation Centre that includes many interesting displays such as entry to the gun's loading area and photographs showing the gun's arrival in Gibraltar. The Battery also boasts a unique and spectacular vantage of Rosia Bay and the adjacent Parson's Lodge Batteries as well as superb views across the Bay and Strait of Gibraltar.

100-Ton Gun

Napier of Magdala Battery
Rosia Road
Gibraltar
Tel. +350 200 40280

E-mail tourism@gibraltar.gi
Open: Monday-Sunday, 9.30am-6.45pm (last entry: 6.15pm)
Price: £1 (free of charge with Nature Reserve ticket)

*Return to the Grand Parade where you should take the cable car to the cable car top station, located on **Signal Hill Battery** 366m above sea level.*

This battery originally mounted nothing more than a 6-pounder cannon, however in 1892 four Quick Loading 6-inch BL guns on Vavasseur pivots were added, two of which had a range of about 9,144m. The southern 6-inch gun emplacement which protected the Bay was located on the site of the present cable car top station and some remnants remain of the north emplacement's mounting mechanism. The positions were updated at various times until World War II when Signal Hill Battery mounted two 3-inch 30-cwt anti-aircraft guns and a 40-mm Bofor.

*Follow the hill down to St Michael's Gate (which marks the top of Charles V Wall) and continue along the path until you reach O'Hara's Road, a steep hill leading up to **Lord Airey's Battery**.*

Together with the adjacent O'Hara's Battery these are the two highest remaining gun positions on the Rock each armed with 9.2-inch Mark X guns on
Mark VII Mountings. Access to this site is now possible by paying presenting
an entry ticket to the Nature Reserve and paying an additional entry fee of
£3.50. Children under the age of 12 can enter free of charge when accompanied by an adult. The site is open 10:00 to 18:00 Monday to Friday but will
usually be closed during the tourist off-season.

The first of these batteries was named after General Sir Richard, Lord Airey
a former governor of Gibraltar who held the dubious distinction of being Lord
Raglan's quartermaster-general during the Crimean War and was involved in
the launch of the Light Brigade during the Battle of Balaclava in 1854. The
battery was originally built in 1891 mounting a 6-inch BL on Vavaseur centre pivot mounting, but was soon upgraded to a 9.2 inch gun with a range
of 26,518m, which effectively closed the gap between Europe and Northern
Africa. The gun was last fired on April 7, 1976, however, it has been allowed
to deteriorate and the gun and supporting mechanisms are now in quite a
dilapidated state. The mounting area immediately below the gun offers some
insight into how the gun operates including the gun's turntable, a shell hoist

and the shell disposal mechanisms, which remain in a reasonable state of repair considering the gun's abandonment some years ago. You can also still see the trolleys used to move shells from the storage area to the loading mechanism. Unfortunately access to the complex of rooms below the battery including the connecting tunnel to O'Hara's Battery is no longer possible.

An external pathway connects Lord Airey's Battery to **O'Hara's Battery** and you will notice a spare 9.2-inch barrel as well as a useful sign providing technical information on the gun at O'Hara's Battery including distance across the Bay, which is 8,230m and the distance across the Straits, which is 23,317m. The underground engine room housed a 10.5 break-horsepower oil engine to drive the shell hoists and linked the two batteries but the door to this area is firmly sealed shut. O'Hara's Battery, which is in much better condition than the adjacent Airey's Battery, is named after James O'Hara, the Second Baron Tyrawley who was governor of Gibraltar in 1756. While Governor of Gibraltar, O'Hara built a tower close to this position in the hope that the few extra metres of elevation would allow him to see the Spanish fleet at Cadiz. Needless to say, his tower offered no such vantage and was nicknamed O'Hara's Folly. It was destroyed by the gunners of composite gunboat HMS Wasp in 1888, who had made a wager with their garrison counterparts that the tower could be destroyed by gunfire from below. The Wasp's 4-inch guns needed only 6 shots to pick it off from its anchor west of the Bay, before sailing off, never to return again to Gibraltar (it sank in Singapore just a few months later).

The guided tour allows access to the well-preserved gun mounting area and control room, which mounts a permanent display of equipment relating to the gun. From its exterior you can clearly see that this gun is in far better condition than the one at Lord Airey's Battery. In particular you will note that the breech and loading mechanisms are still in a near perfect state and many of the parts have been sufficiently greased keeping them moveable. It is said that if the gun had been fired continuously, the ridge on which it is positioned would have been unable to absorb its considerable shock-load, dismounting the gun from its position. Luckily this theory was never tested as the guns saw very little action during the wars.

O'Hara' Battery

Upper Rock, Gibraltar
Tel. +350 200 45957
Open: Monday - Saturday 10:00am-6.00pm during tourist season
£3.50 for a guided tour, free entry for accompanied children under 12

After exiting the area of O'Hara's, return to O'Hara's Road and start your descent. There is a large iron gate on your right hand side that leads to **Breakneck Battery**, which remains MOD property and is completely inaccessible to visitors.

Breakneck Battery most recently mounted a 9.2-inch Mark X gun like the guns on Lord Airey's and O'Hara's Batteries but was abandoned in 1953 and only the protective shield remains today.

Retrace your steps in the direction of Charles V Wall and make your way down all four sections of the wall to the area known as Apes Den.

Queen's Gate, which was cut through the original Spanish wall by the British around 1790, is flanked on either side by the barrels of two 18-ton 10-inch RMLs which have been set into the wall.

Follow the hill to the main area of Ape's Den and here you will see an interesting piece of military engineering known as **Healey's Mortar**, set into the Rock.

This mortar, perhaps more correctly termed a fougasse was first developed by the Knights of St John in Malta in 1740 and consists of a hollowed-out area of solid rock, 1.2m deep and cut at a 45° angle to the horizon. Into this, a large charge of gunpowder was packed together with broken rocks and stones which, when ignited, shot a lethal explosion of debris for a distance of up to 91m with a spread of 549m. It was thought that Healey's Mortar would be a useful defensive weapon in the latter stages of a land assault, but it was only ever fired under test conditions and never effectively used against an enemy.

From Healey's Mortar, follow the hill down towards **Devils Gap Battery**, *a somewhat neglected battery whose use dates back to the Spanish occupation of the Rock when it was known as Punta del Diablo.*

Much of what remains of the Battery was built during the British occupation and during the Great Siege it mainly mounted mortars. The Battery played a valuable part in the defence of Gibraltar during this period and was also active during both World Wars, famously engaging and sinking a German U-Boat in the Bay in 1917. The two 6-inch BL Mk VII coastal defence guns with their own protective steel splinter-shields, which remain in place today, were mounted in the early 20th century replacing two 12cwt QF Mk

I guns. Note the prickly pear cacti in front of the guns, which were planted for the dual purposes of camouflage and as a barrier against enemy infantry attacking soldiers getting to the gun position. The underground complex of buildings to the rear of the southern gun house the original magazine and may also be worthy of exploration. The southern shell hoist remains in a tolerable state of repair although in general the state of the underground complex is not good and you should therefore proceed with caution if venturing to explore it in its entirety.

This walk ends at **Devil's Gap Battery** and you can follow the pedestrian footpath back into town or return to the **Ape's Den** where you can catch the cable car back to the **Grand Parade**. Alternatively you may wish to lengthen your walk by strolling north in the direction of the 5.25-inch AA guns at Princess Anne's Battery (for more information on the guns at Princess Anne's Battery and other guns in their immediate vicinity see Walk 1: Pre-20th-Century British Military History).

– Walk 6 –
Mediterranean Steps and the Upper Rock

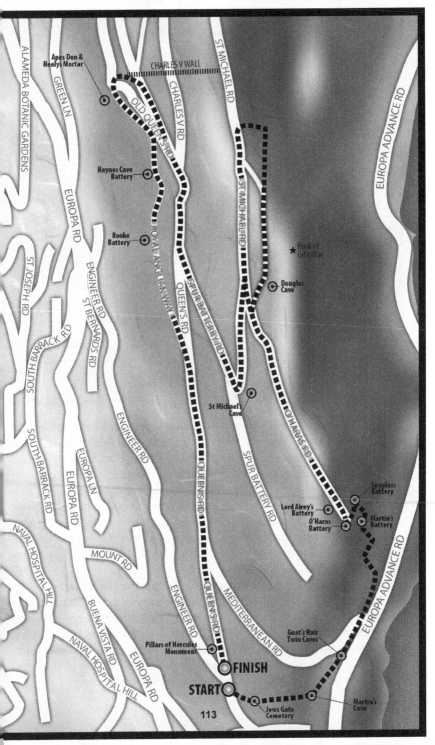

ALAMEDA BOTANIC GARDENS

GREEN LN

CHARLES V WALL

ST MICHAEL RD

OLD QUEEN'S RD

CHARLES V RD

Apes Den & Healys Mortar

EUROPA RD

ST JOSEPH RD

Haynes Cave Battery

Rooke Battery

ROYAL ANGLIAN WAY

QUEEN'S RD

SPUR BATTERY RD

ST MICHAEL RD

ENGINEER RD

ST BERNARD'S RD

SOUTH BARRACK RD

SOUTH BARRACK RD

EUROPA LN

ENGINEER RD

EUROPA RD

★ Rock of Gibraltar

Douglas Cave

EUROPA ADVANCE RD

St Michael's Cave

SPUR BATTERY RD

O'HARAS RD

NAVAL HOSPITAL HILL

MOUNT RD

BUENA VISTA RD

NAVAL HOSPITAL HILL

ENGINEER RD

QUEEN'S RD

EUROPA RD

MEDITERRANEAN RD

Lord Airey's Battery

O'Haras Battery

Spyglass Battery

Martin's Battery

Pillars of Hercules Monument

Goat's Hair Twin Caves

EUROPA ADVANCE RD

FINISH

START

Martin's Cave

Jews Gate Cemetery

113

There is no better place to wonder at Gibraltar's rich and diverse natural history than within the Upper Rock Nature Reserve. The short journey to the Rock's summit takes visitors to the centre of Gibraltar's unique ecosystem with many small mammals, reptiles and amphibians, thousands of insect species and a wealth of plant life including some that cannot be found anywhere else in the world. During autumn, the Upper Rock becomes the perfect place to witness the thousands of migrating birds that cross the Straits on route to Africa from their breeding grounds in Northern Europe. All this without mentioning Gibraltar's most famous inhabitants, the Barbary apes, which are the only wild primates in the whole of Europe.

But the area known as the Nature Reserve offers far more than just wildlife. Its protected status has meant that unlike so many other parts of Gibraltar, many aspects of the Upper Rock's military heritage have been preserved almost untouched since they were decommissioned after World War II. From the rusting remains of centuries-old military hardware to well-preserved anti-aircraft guns from the 1940s, the Upper Rock has so much to offer visitors with even a passing interest in Gibraltar's historical background.

Getting your bearings: This walk begins at the Pillars of Hercules Monument at the entrance to the Upper Rock Nature Reserve and incorporates the walk known as Mediterranean Steps, which will take you to Lord Airey's Battery at the summit before looping down off the beaten track to the start of the walk. Visitors should note that pedestrian entry to the Upper Rock (excluding attractions) costs just 50p as opposed to the full £10 entry that includes all of the Upper Rock attractions such as the Moorish Castle, the Siege Tunnels and St Michael's Cave. If you are driving, you are therefore advised to leave your car outside of the barrier but should be warned that there are very few places to park your car once you have started the steep incline to the Upper Rock via Europa Road. There will also be few opportunities to purchase refreshments during this walk so you should make sure that you take plenty of water, especially during the summer months.

Length: Approximately 3km/1.8mi (4-4.5 hours)

The **Pillars of Hercules Monument** is located on the site of **Jew's Cemetery Battery**, which was the westernmost of the three 9.2 Inch batteries in the area of Windmill Hill. The original battery was constructed in 1891 at a cost of £2,160 and was the first 9.2-inch batteries (Breach Loading as opposed to RML or "Rifled Muzzle Loader") gun to be mounted in Gibraltar. After mounting various calibres of gun during its short life, the gun position at Jew's Cemetery Battery was eventually decommissioned in 1928. The Pillars of Hercules Monument was added in the 1990s and symbolizes Gibraltar's legendary status as the northern pillar of Hercules with either Jebel Musa in Morocco or more likely Monte Hacho in Ceuta, both across the Strait, considered its southern counterpart.

Legend has it that the Pillars were created by the mythical Greek hero Heracles (adapted to Hercules by the Romans). Having been driven mad by the goddess Hera, Hercules killed his wife and children and escaped into the wilderness to consider the gravity of his actions. His cousin Theseus convinced Hercules to visit the Oracle at Delphi who told him that as a penance he would have to perform twelve labours set by King Eurystheus. The tenth labour was to travel to Erytheia to capture the Cattle of Geryon and after completing this labour he split a mountain in two creating a gap from which the Atlantic Ocean could flow and create the Mediterranean Sea. These two mountains were later named Mons Calpe (Gibraltar) and Mons Abila (Jebel Musa or Monte Hacho) by the Romans who nicknamed the gates Non Plus Ultra or "nothing beyond", the end of the known world. Recent excavations of sea caves on the south-eastern side of the Rock have revealed the remains of altars where ancient mariners offered tributes to Hercules and other gods of the day.

On a clear day the lookout provides excellent views across the Strait towards Africa, although unfortunately the temptation to build was too much for one developer who built luxury apartments directly in front of the lookout, partially obscuring the view. There is a small building on the Rock to the rear of the battery. This is a field centre belonging to the Gibraltar Ornithological and Natural History Society (GONHS) and, down the hill from this, a narrow staircase leads up to **Jews Gate Cemetery**. The Cemetery was last used in 1848 but there are graves dating back to the middle of the 18th century. A coloured path charts a route through the centre of the cemetery which provides an interesting snapshot of Gibraltar's past and a static reminder of the important role the Jewish people played in shaping the history of Gibraltar.

*Return to the road and take the path directly behind the GONHS field centre, which is clearly marked **Mediterranean Steps**.*

Mediterranean Steps begins as an enclosed walkway surrounded by trees on either side, but soon opens up into a rocky and upward sloping path, which affords views to Gibraltar's south on the walker's right hand side.

The first spot that is worthy of mention is **Levant Battery**, which you will be able to see a few metres from the path on a south facing ridge on your right hand side about 100m into the walk. The Battery was named as such as it commanded an impressive vantage point over the area of Windmill Hill and

Europa Point below while being positioned low enough not to be obscured by Gibraltar's infamous Levanter cloud, formed by easterly winds and humid conditions. The Battery was built in 1901 and mounted a 9.2-inch BL Mk X on a Mk V mounting, which was still in place with its steel outer shield to protect the gun crew from splinters (albeit in a dilapidated state) as recently as the 1980s but has now been removed for scrap. The gun and Battery saw active service during World War I and on December 31, 1915 fired two rounds at an enemy submarine in the Strait. The path down to the Battery has become quite overgrown and you should proceed with extreme caution if you wish to access it or the magazine and supporting buildings around it. On a ridge about 50m up to the left of the path there is a small and unspectacular observation post known as Fire Control South and you should proceed with similar caution if you wish to climb up to it.

After rising to an apex, the path tails off into a short flight of downwards steps before levelling out for about 150m. The sheer cliffs on your left hand side are known nesting areas for peregrine falcons, which are resident in the Upper Rock and it is also not uncommon to see Barbary partridges in this area. The path soon turns to steps that you are invited to follow on your left

*The more adventurous may wish to deviate from the path slightly at this point and traverse the small wall at the foot of the steps to visit **Martin's Cave**. You should once again proceed with caution at this stage as the path leading to the cave is extremely overgrown and does not have the advantage of handrails like the remainder of the walk.*

There is an abandoned military observation post and the entrance to the cave is via a small opening at the end of a narrow ledge running up the cliff face. This cave is located about 183m above sea level and was only (re)discovered by an artillery soldier in 1821.

During World War II, the cave was used as a generator room but it is now an important roosting and breeding site for the rare Schreiber's Bat and you should therefore **not enter the cave under any circumstances**. The cave was surveyed by the Gibraltar Cave Research Group in November 1966 and a painted sign on the cave's wall marks the occasion. Curiously, former excavations of this cave yielded two swords and a sword belt thought to be of 13th century Berber origin, which are now exhibited at the British Museum in London.

*After returning to the path, follow the first set of steps to the **Goats Hair Twin Caves**, a prominent feature of the Mediterranean Steps.*

Once again a painted sign in the larger cave makes reference to an excavation, this time in 1969, by the Gibraltar Cave Research Group. Excavations at these caves have revealed evidence of the ritual burial of a woman dating back to the Neolithic period and various artefacts relating to these excavations are now on display at the Gibraltar Museum. It is amazing to think that our prehistoric ancestors would have once inhabited these caves, but equally astounding is the fact that these caves would have once been at sea level! The entrance to the Goats Hair Twin Caves make a perfect resting spot but please makes sure that you leave no evidence of your visit by taking all rubbish with you.

After exploring the caves, return to the adjacent steps and continue your ascent. The steps become a little steeper at this point and the handrail becomes a more useful aid. Eventually the path levels off again near a brick building, which is a water-pumping station dating back to World War II. Cross through the nearby tunnel and follow the gently inclining path until you reach **Mediterranean Battery** *(later renamed* **Martin's Battery**)*, built to protect Gibraltar's eastern (Mediterranean) coast from an enemy landing.*

The edge of the Battery at the far extreme offers excellent views of Gibraltar's eastern side including Catalan Bay and on a clear day you can enjoy unobstructed views of Spain's Mediterranean coastline all the way up to Malaga. The Battery was armed in 1834 with a 10-inch brass howitzer and a 24-pounder cannon and later mounted two 7-inch Rifle Breech Loader cannon. During World War II the Battery mounted two 4-inch naval guns and the nearby network of observation points provided auxiliary support to the batteries on the Upper Ridge by providing them with information on enemy targets when their view was obscured by the levanter cloud.

Retrace your steps slightly and continue upwards via the path that lies parallel to the approach way. There is a good 500m of inclined path before you reach the final set of zig-zagged steps that are cut into the limestone and

take you to the summit of the Mediterranean Steps. A seat is carved into the stone near the steps' highest point and will provide a much-needed rest after the final gruelling climb. You will arrive at the summit at the location of **Spy Glass Battery**, *which, at 426m, is the highest point of the Rock.*

Despite its towering position, this battery never fulfilled its full potential and after being mounted with six 10-inch high-angle RMLs (with an enormous amount of difficulty) in 1899, it soon fell into disuse and these were removed in 1907. Just south of Spy Glass Battery and adjacent to the path at the summit of Mediterranean Steps is **Lord**

Airey's Battery. Together with the adjacent **O'Hara's Battery**, they are the two highest remaining gun positions on the Rock each armed with 9.2-inch Mark X guns on Mark VII Mountings (for more information on these guns see Walk 5: Guns of Gibraltar).

You should now begin your descent of O'Hara's Road and will note the view on your left hand side of the Bay of Gibraltar and the industrial port city of Algeciras, Spain's busiest port, which serves as the main embarkation point between Spain and Morocco.

This is also an excellent vantage to observe Gibraltar's dockyard, the pride of the Royal Navy before being passed to the Gibraltar government in the 1980s (for more information on Gibraltar's dockyard see *Walk 4: Naval Gibraltar*).

About three-quarters of the way down O'Hara's Road there is a right turning that leads you to **Douglas Path***, a trail which takes its name from the Douglas Cave, enclosed in the brick shelter at the commencement of the path. The tunnel is shrouded in complete darkness however the use of a torch will reveal a military insignia on the rear wall of the cave. The path continues for about 100m until you reach a military observation point, which, due to its excellent views both of the eastern and western side of the Rock, was the Fortress Commander's command post during World War II.*

There are several water storage tanks and a series of interconnected rooms built into the Rock leading to the east-facing lookout post. On the right hand side of this room, a window leads to a small ledge that despite the inherent dangers (there is no guardrail), offers excellent views of the east side of the Rock. Note for example the small village of Catalan Bay (La Caleta) which was originally populated by Genoese fishermen in the 17th century and is now home to their descendents. Catalan Bay is still the centre of what remains of Gibraltar's fishing industry and one of the most popular beaches on the east side of the Rock as well as being home to several seafood restaurants.

The lookout is also an excellent location from which to appreciate the slope of the ancient sand dune above Sandy Bay. This was in recent times covered with corrugated steel sheets to create a water catchment system for the collection of much needed fresh water for Gibraltar. Work on the **Water Catchments** began in 1903 to provide for the needs of the growing population and a reservoir was excavated into the side of the Rock to store the collected rainwater. Following the construction of two reverse osmosis desalination plants in 1991, the high costs of maintaining the water catchments was no longer justifiable to the British MOD and the water catchments were decommissioned, the surface sheeting removed and the area seeded and allowed to return to its natural habitat.

Return to Douglas Path and follow the steps down to a small structure that many believe to be an early Moorish lookout post and therefore one of the oldest structures on the Upper Rock.

There is evidence to suggest that the stonework is in fact far more recent and that this is therefore more likely to be a British construction; however this does not detract from the secluded beauty of the spot. This area, traditionally known as Mount Misery, was the scene of a Spanish attempt to reclaim Gibraltar just a few months after it had been taken by an Anglo-Dutch force. Guided by a former resident goatherd Simon Susarte, a small force of 500 men led by Colonel de Figueroa climbed to this spot via a path leading from the southern end of the Rock in order to spring a surprise attack on the garrison. Expected support from Spanish and French troops never materialized and when the alarm was raised by a drummer boy who was carrying food to the sentries, the invaders engaged in a bloody battle with the defending Dutch and British force. The attackers had only limited ammunition and without the expected reinforcements most were captured, killed by musket fire or fell to their deaths while trying to escape. English sappers ensured that this already unsteady path could never be used again by scarping large sections of it.

*A small viewing platform adjoins the road leading to the summit of **Charles V Wall** at St Michael's Gate where a small square bastioned fort stood when the wall was first constructed. Despite conflicting accounts from historians, the original structure of the wall was probably built in 1540 during the Spanish occupation of the Rock to repel attacks from Barbary pirates from the south.*

The wall extends beyond these four sections, however the area of the wall below the Apes Den cannot be walked on. The cable car top station is nearby on Signal Hill Battery, which was the site of a windmill built during the Almohad dynasty and which no longer exists. Walkers may be able to purchase refreshments from here *or alternatively follow the path in the opposite direction down to St Michael's Cabin, a snack-bar and cafeteria with a gift shop located near St Michael's Cave*. St Michael's cave is a natural grotto situated about 300m above sea level and is probably Gibraltar's oldest tourist attraction with its caverns and galleries having appealed to visitors to the Rock as far back as the Roman occupation of the Iberian Peninsular.

The Cave provides an excellent view of the Rock's interior and nowadays hosts Classical Music concerts. These are well-worth attending if the opportunity arises, not only for the uniqueness of the setting but also for the excellent acoustics the Cave provides. The main or Cathedral cave, which is open to visitors, consists of an upper hall followed by a series of smaller halls and chambers dropping to depths of approximately 76m below the entrance level. A fallen stalagmite at the far end of the main Chamber offers a close-up view of a centuries old natural phenomenon. During World War II the Cave was set up for use as a hospital. While it was barely used as such, it was at this time, while blasting an alternative entrance to the cave, that the series of caves known as Lower St Michael's Cave was found. Lower St Michael's Cave is accessible but only by pre-arranging a tour with an official guide (see page 177 Tours for further details on tours of Lower St Michael's Cave).

St Michael's Cave
St Michael's Road
Upper Rock
Gibraltar

Open: Monday-Sunday, 9.30am-7pm
Prices: Entry to the Upper Rock Nature Reserve costs £10 (adults) and £5
(children) and includes St Michael's Cave, City Under Siege Exhibition, the
Moorish Castle and the Great Siege Tunnels

From St Michael's Cave you should make your descent via the steep (and
unmarked!) Cave Branch Road. When the road levels out continue until you
reach a fork in the road and follow the central path onto Queen's Road until
you reach Charles V Wall where a picnic area has been built on the site of an
old battery. Here you can choose to take an approximate 1.5-hour diversion
*along the beautiful **Inglis Way**, which can be reached by following the rocky*
path on the right adjacent to the road.

This path may have been named after a member of the armed forces who was
stationed in Gibraltar in the 19th century, although it is more likely to have
derived from the Spanish for "Englishman's Path", el camino del Ingles.

Ascending the path you will see a World War II searchlight position with
auxiliary buildings including a half cylindrical steel Nissen hut with a concrete
roof. Further up the path, before you reach the concrete road marked by a
green water storage tank, the route veers off to the left.

This is probably the best place in the Upper Rock to observe what little remains of the so-called **Moorish Wall** (also known as Philip II Wall or Muralla de San Raymondo during the Spanish occupation of the Rock), which would have run from the South Demi-Bastion in the town area up the western face of the Rock to Signal Hill, protecting the city from attacks from the south. Much of the wall, which is mainly Spanish-built (probably designed by Italian Engineer Juan Baustista Calvi in the early 16th century) over the original Moorish structure, has been destroyed down the years and what remains is largely obscured by dense scrub. Nevertheless it is possible from this point to observe the wall's masonry as well as getting an indication of its original height and breadth as you cut through it in continuation of the walk.

The path continues beyond the Wall for about 0.6m (1km) and what it lacks in military architecture it certainly makes up for in natural beauty.

The canopy is predominantly made up of olive trees and the shade that these trees provide is conducive to an interesting array of plants and flowers such as the beautiful purple Jerusalem sage as well as some of Gibraltar's rare orchids.

The walk takes you past two World War II observation posts and some concrete water catchments before arriving at the old abandoned MOD Nursery. Rather than continue the path uphill along the Nursery's fence, it would be best to retrace your route back along Inglis Way and return to Charles V Wall.

*Continue down the final stretch of Charles V Wall as it emerges near the **Apes Den** in the area of Queen's Gate, a gate cut through the originally Spanish wall by the British around 1790.*

Plans of the Rock's fortifications from the 16th century suggest that Charles V Wall would have been connected to the more northerly Moorish Wall at this point by way of a straight fortified wall, however there are no visible remains of this structure today. The **Apes Den** is where one of five troops of Barbary macaques that live in the Upper Rock reside, making up the total population of around 240 monkeys. The Gibraltar macaques are the only wild population of monkeys in Europe and some believe they may be a remnant of populations that had spread throughout southern Europe millions of years ago when the Mediterranean had dried up creating a land ridge to Africa.

Others still speak of a legendary subterranean tunnel beginning at Lower St Michael's Cave, which connects Gibraltar to Africa under the Strait of Gibraltar. Unglamorous though it may sound, the most likely explanation is that the macaques were introduced by the North African inhabitants of the Rock who would have originally brought them across the Strait to keep them as pets.

Another urban legend, though one which is taken very seriously round these parts, is that as long as the macaques remain on the Rock, Gibraltar will continue to be British. Foreign and Commonwealth Office documents recently released to the British National Archives revealed just how much attention has historically been paid to the health and welfare of the macaques. These files revealed that Winston Churchill himself had taken a personal interest in them during World War II, insisting that the population which had dwindled to just a few individuals be increased to a minimum of 24 macaques, and that this number be maintained from then on.

Care of the macaques passed from the Gibraltar Regiment (who appointed an officer to supervise their care) to the Gibraltar Government in 1991 and they are now cared for by the GONHS who ensure that they are healthy and well fed. You are therefore advised to not, under any circumstances, offer them any food. Furthermore, you should remember that the macaques are semi-wild animals and not household pets so it follows that stroking them or touching them in any way is strictly off-limits.

*Take the short slope down to the Apes Den where you can see **Healey's Mortar** set into the Rock nearby.*

Healey's Mortar is an improvised mine dating back to the 18th century, which was constructed by making a hollow in the Rock and filling this with explosives (see Walk 5: The Guns of Gibraltar).

*You can now either take the short detour down to **Devil's Gap Battery** (see Walk 5: The Guns of Gibraltar) or cross through **Queen's Gate** and begin your ascent of Old Queen's Road.*

You will see various metal rings intermittently placed on the side of the road that were used to pull cannons and other heavy equipment to their locations on the Upper Rock. On close inspection you may find bullet casings in the gutters at the sides of the roads in the Upper Rock. These belong to blank ammunition fired by the Gibraltar Regiment while on regular exercise in the Upper Rock and for your own safety you are advised to leave any such casings where you find them.

*After ascending Old Queen's Road for about 50m, there is a turning on the right hand side leading to **Royal Anglian Way**.*

This pathway was constructed in 1969 by the soldiers of the 2nd Battalion of the Royal Anglian Regiment and is still maintained by them today with the help of the Gibraltar Regiment. The path leads to two derelict batteries, the first one being **Haynes Cave Battery**, named after Captain Haynes, who was the Garrison's quartermaster in 1787—around the time when this battery first mounted guns. The battery presently consists of twin mounts with the barrel and shield of one of the 4-inch QF guns still on view on the southern mount. Having been completed in its present form in 1904, the battery was decommissioned in 1911 with its function taken over by the larger 6-inch guns at Tovey Battery. The area at the northern end of Royal Anglian Way doubles as a feeding area for the Anglian Way macaque troop and is a good spot for observing them in their natural environment, free from the hordes of tourists that tend to frequent the Apes Den.

As you follow the path, you will notice several interesting structures including former military kitchens, recognizable by the elongated ceramic chimneys that extend from them up the side of the Rock. Continue along the path, which reaches a short flight of steps leading to Rooke Battery.

This battery was named after Admiral Sir George Rooke who commanded the allied naval forces in the capture of Gibraltar in 1704 and went on to became its first governor. It was built in 1907 and mounted a 9.2-inch BL Mark X gun on a Mark V mounting similar to the guns at Lord Airey's and O'Hara's Batteries. However this gun was removed in 1928 and the position was used as the Fire Command Headquarters and an electric searchlight was mounted during World War II. This searchlight would have been able to throw a concentrated beam of light three degrees wide on a ship up to a range of 1.2mi (2km). The remains of the searchlight position built upon the original gun mounting can still be seen.

Follow the hill up to Queens Road, which was named after Queen Elizabeth II (much to the infuriation of the Spanish) visited Gibraltar in 1954 as part of her Commonwealth Tour. A marble plaque at the look-out 100m up the road, marks the spot where she stopped to take a view of the town. Continue down from here to the Pillars of Hercules monument near Jews Gate, where the walk began and now ends.

– Walk 7 –
The Defensive Fortifications of Gibraltar

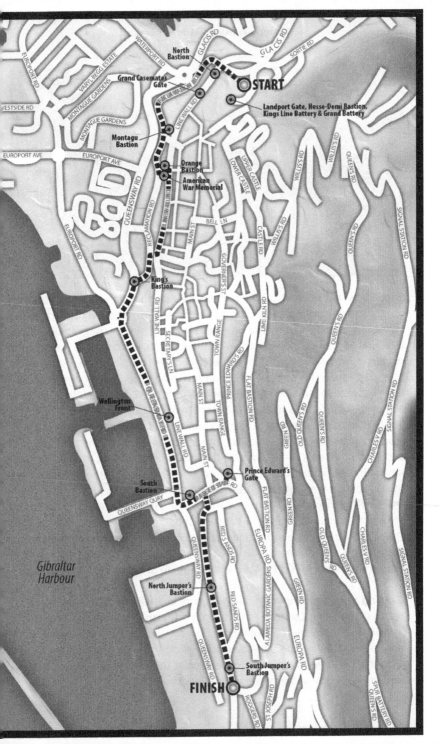

Shaped by nature and complemented by human ingenuity, Gibraltar has rightly gained the reputation for being one of the world's most formidable fortresses. Surrounded by sea on three sides and almost completely without a natural anchorage, only a narrow isthmus connects Gibraltar to the Spanish mainland; a solitary land approach presided over by the Rock's insurmountable north face. Its strategic location has made Gibraltar a much sought-after possession since the Berber general Tariq ibn-Ziyad used the Rock as a stepping-stone for the invasion of Europe in AD 711. Gibraltar was a prize the Muslims were not willing to relinquish and it was said to have been Tariq who built the city's first walls, which were to be enhanced over time by his Muslim successors. When Gibraltar finally fell into Spanish hands, the Rock's new inhabitants knew that the city's fortifications needed to be improved, and this job was undertaken with the assistance of prominent Italian Engineers. When the British arrived in 1704 they further modernized the existing defensive structures bringing them up-to-date with modern siege warfare. The changes that Gibraltar's walls and bastions have undergone over the centuries make Gibraltar the ideal place to marvel at the development of defensive fortifications from the early Middle Ages all the way up to World War II.

Getting your bearings: This walk begins at Landport Gate, which can be reached by exiting Casemates Square on its north-eastern side, through the walkway beneath the Casemates Barracks (next to the Lord Nelson pub) and then continuing through Landport Tunnel. The walk traverses the city of Gibraltar via its walls and bastions, ending at the area of Parson's Lodge Battery on the south-western side of the Rock.

Length: Approximately 3km/1.8mi (2.5 hours)

The Landport Defences are best appreciated in the context of the defensive fortifications that surround it.

*After exiting **Landport Gate**, cross the timber drawbridge and turn to face the Gate, which marks the position of the original medieval gate that would for a time have been the only entrance into the city of Gibraltar other than by sea.*

The gate was improved by the Spanish around 1543 and a defensive ditch was dug at the base of the wall at this time, with a stone bridge being added some years later. Much of the Spanish construction was destroyed during the Thirteenth Siege of Gibraltar in 1727 and was rebuilt in largely its present form by the British after that date. Fifty years later, during the Great Siege, the British decided to do away with the stone bridge at Landport and replaced it with a moveable timber drawbridge.

Looking up towards the Rock from the drawbridge you will note the proximity of the Tower of Homage and the outer wall of the Moorish Castle zigzagging down from the Tower to the **6th and 7th Crutchett's Batteries**. The batteries above the 6th and 7th Crutchett's Batteries are known as the **Castle Batteries** and have been constructed en Crémaillère referring to the angled parapet that ensures an oblique as well as a direct line of fire while also offering shelter from the enemy's flanking fire. Much of what remain of these defences is British-built, although remnants of the anterior Spanish walls can be seen on the lower parts of the walls where the brickwork differs. Like many of Gibraltar's defences, the Spanish lines were built on almost the exact position of the original Merinid walls, parts of which also still remain and can be observed more closely from the 1st and 2nd Castle Batteries nearest the Tower.

Adjacent to Landport Gate on its eastern side is **Hesse's Demi-bastion** built in 1730 on the site of the Spanish St.Peter's Bastion (Baluado de San Pedro). This bastion was named after Prince George of Hesse-Darmstadt under whose command British and Dutch marines took the fortress of Gibraltar in 1704 and defended it against subsequent attacks from Spanish-French forces. Despite his key role in the development of Gibraltar's history, Prince George's importance is often diminished in contemporary accounts of the taking of Gibraltar with Admiral Sir George Rooke often given major credit and recognition for Gibraltar's capture. Immediately behind Hesse's Demi-bastion is **King's Lines Battery**, named after Archduke Charles of Austria who was pretender to the Spanish throne as King Charles III of Spain and **Bombproof Battery** lies directly behind that. These batteries link the Castle Batteries to the Kings Lines and the area known as the Northern Defences. The battery that stands to your rear is the aptly named **Couvreporte Battery**, which covers the door or porte to the town. This modestly sized but important battery was built in 1761 and had three embrasures for guns that were later upgraded to accommodate anti-tank weaponry during World War II.

Follow the recently built wooden staircase down into Landport ditch, which is now used as a car parking area. The large battery that flanks the car park on its southern side and into which Landport Gate is essentially cut is **Grand**

Battery, which was built to defend Gibraltar's only land front. This battery, also built along the line of the original medieval wall, was rebuilt by the Spanish and named the Wall of Saint Bernard (Muralla de San Bernando). After being severely damaged during the Anglo-Dutch bombardment of 1704 the present broader wall was built by the British. Before the advent of long range artillery, the city's northern end was naturally the most vulnerable to attack. It therefore follows that the fortifications defending this part of the city are among the most comprehensive. In addition to flanking fire from both sides, potential attackers would also have had to negotiate an inundation (where the Laguna housing estate is now situated) as well as minefields and the aforementioned ditch before even reaching the 15 gun embrasures of the Grand Battery itself.

*Continue west along the Grand Battery under Smith Dorrien Bridge and you will arrive at the **North Bastion**, the first of several formidable bastions that line Gibraltar's western side.*

This bastion is built on the site of a square tower known as the Giralda Tower, which was built in 1309. While The Giralda Tower's high battlements and square indentations were suitable for archers, the Tower was not apt for mounting cannon and a smaller square platform known as the Bulwark of Saint Paul (San Pablo) was built on this spot by the Spanish. A glacis (an artificial slope made of earth) extending northwards in the direction of the inundation roughly where the Glacis housing estate now stands, provided a further line of protection. The bastion, which was vastly improved by the British, not only defended the north-western corner of the town, it also provided flanking fire across the Grand Battery and supported the Montagu and Orange Bastions that protected the city from amphibious assaults from the west. A counterguard covers the bastion on its western side and the area between the counterguard and the bastion was a troop assembly point known as **West Place of Arms**. Much of this area is now occupied by a used car dealer and you will note adjacent to its forecourt a small fountain set into the wall. This was erected by an unnamed animal lover in 1934 and was used until fairly recently as a watering trough for horses.

Continue between the bastion and the counterguard in the direction of the public market until you arrive at Waterport Plaza, a small square with a clock tower known colloquially as Plaza del Reloj, which now doubles as Gibraltar's bus terminus.

Grand Casemates Gate leads into Casemates Square and was originally built in 1727 on the site of the original Water Gate from which the medieval inhabitants of the Rock launched their galleys. An extra gate was cut into the line wall in 1884 to assist with the increased traffic flow in the town area and a break in the opposing counterguard was also made some years later for the same reason.

Follow Fish Market Lane between the Public Market and the interior of Montagu Counterguard. Montagu Counterguard provides defensive cover for **Montagu Bastion***, a powerful bastion that can be best viewed where Fish Market Lane curves at a 90 degree angle to the left.*

The Bastion, positioned on the site of the Spanish Platform of Saint Andrew was named after Ralph Montagu, the First Duke of Montagu. It is a large five-sided bastion that was originally constructed around 1740 but was built in its present shape in 1773. By 1859 it had become arguably the mightiest of Gibraltar's fortifications, mounting 29 guns that mainly offered protection to the mole in its foreground. In 1868 three 10-inch, 18-ton RMLs were added together with iron shielded emplacements that can still be seen today. Montagu Bastion was used as an anti-aircraft position during World War II when the bastion mounted 3.7-inch anti-aircraft guns.

Montagu Bastion is connected to Orange Bastion by a curtain wall known as Montagu Curtain which has three gun embrasures either side of a well preserved gate dating to the late 18th century. The larger gap in the curtain, south of the wooden gate was added at a later date, once again to assist with traffic-flow problems. Opposite this gate, a large unsightly block of flats has been built on a breach between the Montagu Counterguard and Chatham Counterguard. Chatham Counterguard was named after John Pitt, the Second Earl of Chatham who was governor of Gibraltar from 1820 to 1835.

*Follow the path between Chatham Counterguard and Orange Bastion and you will notice that the casemates of the counterguard on your right hand side have been restored to use as shop units. The curve in the road takes you around Orange Bastion to Prince Albert's Front and the **American War Memorial**.*

The archway and steps that blend into the original limestone-coursed ashlar wall were commissioned by the American Battle Commission in 1932 to commemorate the co-operation of American and British Forces at Gibraltar during World War I. There are two plaques mounted nearby, the first commemorates the arrival of the first American naval squadron to Gibraltar in 1801. The second, a more recent addition, commemorates Operation Torch, the Allied invasion of North Africa in November 1942, which was launched and commanded from Gibraltar.

*Follow the so-called "American Steps" onto **Line Wall Curtain**, which, like so many other walls in Gibraltar, was built roughly on the site of the original medieval sea wall. The actual Line Wall stretches beyond South Bastion up to Engineer Battery to the south of the town, however the road known nowadays as Line Wall is that which extends between the North and South bastions. On your left hand side as you come to the top of the steps you will see two 32-pounders on a south facing embrasure and a further two facing north on the right hand side of the bastion.*

You are standing on the former St Anne's Platform, now **Orange Bastion** and named after William III of England who was Prince of Orange by birth. This curiously shaped bastion was, like Montagu Bastion, modernized in the late 19th century to encompass a heavy RML battery with iron shields. It mounted two 10-inch, 18-ton RMLs during this time, and barrels have recently been restored to this position offering a nostalgic view of what the bastion might have looked like in Victorian times. From the bastion's left flank you can see a further four cannons on Chatham Counterguard facing south and west, these are a mix of 32- and 24-pounders on modern carriages that were placed here during a recent renovation of the city's defences.

Follow the short staircase onto **Prince Albert's Front**, *which lies parallel to Line Wall Road.*

This defensive wall runs between Orange Bastion and King's Bastion and is the site of a former saluting battery. Prince Albert's Front, named after Queen Victoria's husband, the Prince Consort, was restored for use as a car parking area and built on quite extensively, including the Community Centre built at the far end of the wall on **Zoca Flank Battery**. The word Zoca is thought to have derived from the Arabic word zoco or souq, which referred to the market that would have stood in close proximity. Of particular note on this stretch of the line wall is an 18th-century expense magazine and various sets of small steps (known as banquettes) that allowed the protecting forces to fire over the crest of the parapet. The large white building on your left hand side as you walk south along Prince Albert's Front conceals the remnants of an Islamic tower and the original line wall in its basement. However, these are unfortunately inaccessible to the general public.

Descend the steps from Prince Albert's Front onto **Line Wall Promenade**, *an area cut from the city walls in 1921 during the Governorship of General Sir Horace Smith-Dorrien. Immediately on your right hand side at the base of the steps is a small disused fountain set into the wall of the bastion.*

This fountain, which was supplied by an aqueduct, was built in 1571 and was originally situated in the Piazza adjacent to the building that is now the City

Hall (near Fountain Ramp, which took its name). The fountain was moved to Castle Street at the end of the 19th century and continued to be in use until it was moved to its present location in 1967. In the centre of the Promenade is the **City War Memorial**, which was erected in 1923 by public subscription at the cost of £1,700. This memorial was sculpted from Carrara marble by Catalan Sculptor Jose Piquet Catoli and commemorates those Gibraltarians who died during World War I. The memorial and steps are flanked on either side by Russian guns 24-pounder cannons that had been captured by the British during the Crimean War and given as a gift to the people of Gibraltar.

Kings Bastion lies at the southern end of the Promenade, and a plaque at the far end commemorates the life of General Sir Robert Boyd, a former governor of Gibraltar who helped design the King's Bastion and whose body is interred in a special chamber built within the bastion walls.

*Return to the centre of the promenade and follow the steps down to Reclamation Road, which leads to the entry to **Kings Bastion** itself.*

Kings Bastion is perhaps the grandest of all of Gibraltar's fortifications and built on the site of the former Platform of Saint Lawrence its location was key in the protection of the city, standing as it does in the foreground of the Cathedral of St Mary the Crowned. Although the idea of a bastion on this site was originally proposed by Colonel Skinner in 1758, it was Chief Engineer William Green who designed the bastion in 1773 with the assistance of the aforementioned Boyd.

The Bastion, with its parapets of solid masonry up to 4.5-m thick and a not insignificant armament of twelve 32-pounders and ten 10-inch howitzers just on its front, was General Eliott's command post during the Great Siege. There are various displays about the bastion's history on the entry tunnel and many of the original building plans are on show at the internet zone at the southern end of the Bastion. You will also be able to see arched cooking areas at the interior of the entry tunnel, with carved ducts to carry away the fumes. The armoured casemates on the top floor of the Bastion once housed heavy duty weaponry but now house a wine bar and disco (for more information on the guns mounted on the Kings Bastion, see *Walk 5: The Guns of Gibraltar*).

The bastion was decommissioned in the early 1900s and soon fell into neglect with the internal areas being used by the Public Works Department and a generating station built onto its northern side in the 1960s. The generating station was demolished in 2005 revealing the bastion's attractive façade for the first time in almost half a century. Kings Bastion took on a new lease of life in 2007 when the building was elegantly renovated making way for a bowling alley, ice-skating rink as well as a multi-screen cinema and other leisure facilities. A particular quality of the leisure centre is the tasteful way in which many aspects of the bastion's original character have been restored to their original glory. In particular the casemated gun emplacements on the roof with guns flanking to the Bastion's left and right side are worthy of a visit, giving a very good impression of what the Bastion would have looked like in the late 18th century. The defences were improved at the end of the 19th century and armoured casemates were added. The barrels of the 12.5-inch, 38-ton and 10-inch, 18-ton RMLs guns that guard the front of the Bastion give some indication of the firing power this Bastion would have had at that time.

After exiting Kings Bastion, walk around the edge of the bastion onto Queensway, a road that was renamed when Queen Elizabeth II visited Gibraltar in 1954 as part of her Commonwealth Tour.

Most of the land outside of the city walls has been reclaimed from the sea during the last century and most of these east-facing bastions were built to protect the city from amphibious assaults. You can now observe an exterior view of Kings Bastion's gun positions and in particular the curved front shield and double gun port of the large central gun.

*Follow Queensway for about 100m and turn left through a narrow passageway that leads to a large car parking area. A narrow flight of steps at the centre of this leads onto **Sir Herbert Miles Boulevard**, a walkway cut into the line wall that was named after Sir Herbert Scott Miles, governor of Gibraltar from 1913 to 1918.*

The Boulevard provides an excellent vantage point to observe the southern flank of Kings Bastion as well as the right flank of Wellington Front's right bastion.

Turn right and walk to the southern end of the boulevard where a small mosque has been named after Tariq Ibn Ziyad, the Berber general who landed on the Rock in AD 711. Follow the short flight of stairs which leads onto a winding road called Lover's Lane which is flanked on its left hand side by Duke of Kent House which was once used as an officer' mess but was more recently Fortress HQ on the Rock.

You will immediately get a view of the rear of *Wellington Front* which was named after Field Marshal Arthur Wellesley, the first Duke of Wellington. With accommodation at such a premium in Gibraltar, it is essential that the city's fortifications are used to their maximum potential. While their use may perhaps detract slightly from its original splendour, Wellington Front houses many clubs and societies within its casemates. Access onto the curtain wall is no longer possible though you can observe many of the wall's original features from the road, including several 18th-century buildings and platforms from where soldiers would have fired their muskets. Wellington Front originally consisted of just a long curtain wall with the bastions at either end added in 1845. In 1878 additions were made to the right bastion in order to mount a single 12.5-inch 36-ton RML together with protective curve shield similar to that of Kings Bastion.

Descend via the southern ramp onto the foot of Wellington Front and cut through the pedestrian access below the Left Bastion to return onto Queensway. Turn south (left) and continue walking for about 50m until you reach **South Bastion***.*

This bastion, which marked the southern limits of the old town, was originally named Señora del Rosario and was built in 1535 by a team of Italian engineers led by architect Benedetto da Ravenna, a contemporary of Leonardo Da Vinci. The British completed the previously incomplete works in the 18th century and the merging of the original Spanish bastion with the British limestone ashlar finish is clearly visible on the bastion's left flank together with 15 loopholes for muskets. In 1859 South Bastion mounted a total of twenty-seven guns, mainly 32-pounders, but like many of the other bastions along the seafront these made way to accommodate a single, heavier 10-inch, 18-ton RML battery. There were three RMLs added in 1881 and these were protected by iron and teak armour plates known as Gibraltar shields, which could withstand ten rounds of fire from a 15-inch gun at a range of 366m without penetrating the iron.

Ragged Staff Flank continues the line of South Bastion on its southern side and two pedestrian as well as a further large vehicular gate have been cut into it, complementing the original single gate. This gate was defended by two 32-Pounder cannons and a guardroom that is no longer present. The dockyard's impressive North Gate stood adjacent to the Ragged Staff Gates on the exterior of the city walls but unfortunately this original stone building was demolished overnight and without public consultation in the early 1990s in order to widen the dockyard's access road. A small plaque at the entrance

to the gate claims that the origin of the name Ragged Staff is unknown, however it has been suggested it is a nautical term for a stump mast fitted to boats and used to hoist provisions on board.

Continue up on Ragged Staff Road and follow the edge of South Bastion up to the statue of Admiral Lord Nelson, which was erected in October 2005 to mark the 200-year anniversary of the Battle of Trafalgar. Using the pedestrian crossing, make your way to the Trafalgar Cemetery (for more information on Trafalgar Cemetery see Walk 4: Naval Gibraltar*) on the opposite side of the road and walk along the Cemetery's exterior wall until you reach another break in the curtain wall known as* **Prince Edward's Gate**.

This gate was named after the fourth son of George III (the father of Queen Victoria) who was stationed in Gibraltar at the time the gate was cut. The steep wall adjacent to the exterior of Prince Edward's Gate is the western flank of **Flat Bastion**, a bastion named as such because, unlike most, it was constructed with a flat face. Originally named Bastion Santiago or Bastion San Jago, Flat Bastion was built by the Spanish in 1552 near the Puerta de Africa or Africa Gate. Like the adjacent South Bastion, the Flat Bastion was never completed by the Spanish and although it mounted five 32-pounder cannons in 1863 its importance to the British soon diminished as the West Side batteries were further developed. Flat Bastion Magazine was designed to hold around 5,000 barrels of gunpowder but now houses a Geological Research Station, which, as well as housing many interesting geological exhibits, allows visitors the chance to to investigate the well-maintained interior of the magazine. There are plans to open this site to the general public but at present the magazine can only be visited by way of guided tour, by contacting F. Gomez (+350 200 44460) or P Hodkinson (+350 200 43910).

The next series of batteries are the West Side batteries, which can be reached by walking south from Prince Edward's Gate in the direction of the Grand Parade, a large former parade ground now used as a car park. Keep the Queens Hotel on your right hand side as you cross the road that leads to the Piccadilly restaurant on Ragged Staff Flank. Follow the line of the wall and continue in a southerly direction, keeping the Alameda housing estate on your left hand side.

This housing estate was built on the site of the Prince of Wales Batteries and Lines and Lady Augusta's Battery is now buried under court no.5 of the nearby Sandpits Lawn Tennis Club. Very little remains of these important defensive fortifications today. Victoria Battery, which is also partially buried beneath this housing estate, was to be important later as its right flank was to mount one of Gibraltar's two 100-ton guns (the other being at Napier of Magadala Battery). The Gibraltar Fire Brigade's headquarters are now located on the right flank of Victoria Battery and its underground network of tunnels are still used by them during training exercises.

The wall you are standing on is the Saluting Battery, known locally as la bateria. There are 21 embrasures cut into the parapet of the wall and you will notice two of the original magazine stores remaining along its length. A stone vent tower with a conical roof (reconstructed by the Spanish) for an underground Moorish aqueduct that runs to the area of the Piazza can also

be seen on the parallel Rosia Road. **North Jumper's Bastion** protects the northern end of the wall and this bastion was originally designed by the Florentine Military architect Giovan Giacomo Paleari Fratino in 1575. It was called Bastion Santa Cruz and in strict military terms the current bastion, re-built by the British in 1785, is actually a demi-bastion as it only has one face. The bombproof casemated barracks below used to provide accommodation for about 200 men and now houses various clubs and a gymnasium as well as a very popular seafood restaurant on its front face (Jumper's Wheel Restaurant).

If North Jumpers Bastion is a testament to the tasteful and efficient modern usage of decommissioned military fortifications in Gibraltar, then the **South Jumpers Bastion** is the complete opposite. Also rebuilt in 1785 on the location of an old sea gate, it is a flat bastion but was designed to only accommodate musket fire as larger guns were by this time already being mounted on retired batteries. The interior of the bastion, which can be viewed from above, is in an advanced state of dilapidation and may now possibly be beyond renovation and use. Both of these bastions were named after Captain Sir William Jumper who was the first Royal Navy officer to come ashore in Gibraltar during the Anglo-Dutch attack of 1704.

The original Moorish and later the Spanish lines used to follow the natural curve of the bay towards the head of the New Mole, which was constructed in 1626. At this point the Tower of *El Tuerto* (the one-eyed man) and the attached fort of the same name offered flanking protection to the walls beyond the South Front. Sadly what remained of these fortifications has now been concealed beneath the various dockyard extensions. While there are some remnants of the **Cumberland and Scud Hill Batteries** just beyond the

BP petrol station, the majority of these have been covered by 20th-century constructions.

Although the walk ends here, you may continue along the sea wall alongside the West Side and Rosia batteries and past **Napier of Magdala Battery** *(home of the 100-ton gun) and* **Parson's Lodge Battery** *all the way to the batteries and fortifications at Europa Point.*

– Walk 8 –
The Great British
Pub Crawl

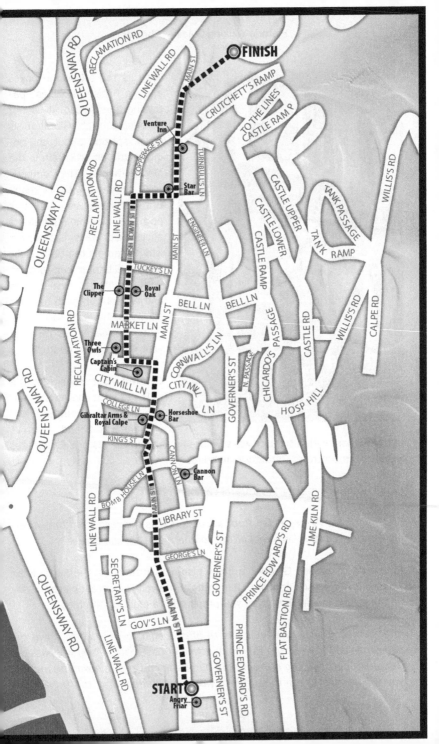

With its red telephone boxes and its British "Bobbies" patrolling the street, it is not surprising that Gibraltar is often spoken about as being a little bit of Britain in the Mediterranean. The comparisons continue with its many British-style pubs, and this pub crawl within Gibraltar's ancient city walls, is a perfect way to sample the best public houses Gibraltar has to offer. With traditional British ales and typical pub grub on offer all along the way, follow this route to make the most of your evening on the Rock.

Getting your bearings: The walk starts at the Angry Friar Pub near the southern end of Main Street and visits 11 pubs and bars within the city walls before finishing in the historic Casemates Square: the centre of Gibraltar's nightlife.

Length: Approximately 1.5km/1mi (2 hours)

*Start off at the **Angry Friar Pub**, situated across the road from the Governor's residence (the Convent) at the southern end of Main Street.*

After a day exploring Gibraltar's many historical attractions, the Angry Friar, which offers al fresco drinking 12 months of the year, is a great place to soak up the last of the sun's rays as you prepare for a night on the tiles.

After sampling what the Friar has to offer, begin to walk north down the pedestrianized Main Street (in the direction of Casemates). You will pass the Gibraltar Court building on your right hand side and after a few more metres, you will be able to see the eastern wall of the Cathedral of the Holy Trinity as you pass through Cathedral Square. You must continue to walk until you reach the Roman Catholic Cathedral of St Mary the Crowned and from here take a right turning onto Cannon Lane (the lane that lies between the Cathedral and Marks and Spencer). You will not be able to miss the **Cannon Bar** *about 20m up the road, adjacent to some 18th-century Officer's Quarters that are now a private dwelling house.*

If you have already taken *Walk 5: Guns of Gibraltar* you will no doubt agree that it is fitting for this traditional-style pub to commemorate the extensive array of armaments that can be seen on the bastions and batteries around Rock.

After enjoying a pint of beer at the Cannon Bar, make your way back down Cannon Lane and turn right onto Main Street. Just beyond the Cathedral of the St Mary the Crowned, on the left hand side of the road and separated by only a few metres of shop front are **the Gibraltar Arms** *and* **the Royal Calpe**.

Both have a small number of tables on Main Street offering an opportunity to people-watch among the hustle and bustle of Gibraltar's city centre. If you wish to enjoy a more relaxing beverage, the recently renovated Royal Calpe also benefits from a conservatory area and beer garden at its rear. This public house takes its name from the Calpe Hunt, which was the name given to a fox hunt that used to be held twice a week during the hunting season of November to March in nearby Spain by the officers of the Garrison until about the end of 19th century.

After exiting the Royal Calpe, take a left turn and continue to walk north on Main Street, until you soon come across the **Horseshoe Bar**.

This bar, which becomes literally packed to the rafters when there is a navy vessel in port, has been the favourite haunt of sailors visiting the Rock for decades. The interior decor has barely changed in years and the Horseshoe remains one of Gibraltar's most authentic British-style Pubs.

As you exit the Horseshoe, turn right and continue north on Main Street for a few steps before taking a left turn onto John Mackintosh Square (the Piazza). Adjacent to the House of Assembly building, on your left hand side you will find the **Captain's Cabin***, which, due to its proximity to the British Naval Base at HMS Rooke is another favourite for visiting sailors.*

After enjoying a swift ale with the Captain, stumble across the Piazza on to Irish Town. This street, which runs parallel to Main Street is easily recognizable by the large orange-bricked Victorian Police Station that marks its southern end. One of the first establishments you will come across on the left hand side of Irish Town is the popular **Three Owls Pub**, *which is set over three floors.*

The first and second floors double as pool halls and most evenings tend to attract a serious pool-playing crowd. On Friday nights however, the Three Owls is the focus for a younger and more alternative crowd who are attracted to the pub by the promise of cheap drinks during the establishment's happy hour. The ground floor still retains many of the characteristics of the original Three Owls pub and has a pool table of its own for those who fancy a less serious game.

Returning back onto Irish Town and turning left, you will soon arrive at the **Clipper bar***.*

Decorated with sailing and naval memorabilia, the Clipper is a favourite among Gibraltarians who tend to be attracted to it during daylight hours due to the fine culinary standards it maintains as well as the modest though excellent selection of beers and traditional ales on tap.

Across the road from the Clipper is possibly the smallest pub on this Crawl, **the Royal Oak***.*

This bar has changed very little down the years but still manages to attract a steady clientele of punters keen to make the most of some of the most inexpensive bar prices within the city walls. If you were unable to get a game at the Three Owls you may be pleased to hear that despite its small size, the proprietors of the Royal Oak have somehow managed to fit in a pool table.

It may be time to soak up some of the alcohol in your bloodstream. Tuckey's Lane, which lies adjacent to Sacarello's Coffee House, leads to another Gibraltar institution, the Maharaja Curry House. The Maharaja has a fully licensed bar as well as some of the best Indian cuisine on the Rock at what must certainly be the most reasonable prices. If a curry is not to your liking, continue your route south on Irish Town and turn right onto Parliament Lane where you will soon chance upon Gibraltar's oldest pub, the Star Bar. Famed for its breakfasts, the **Star Bar** also offers a traditional British alternative to the Maharaja's Indian fare.

Turn left out of the Star Bar and follow Parliament Lane until you reach Main Street. Turning left again you will soon see the bright lights of Casemates Square in the distance. However, before reaching Casemates, where the pub crawl ends, you may wish to stop in on the **Venture Inn** *at the foot of Crutchett's Ramp.*

On Friday and Saturday nights, the Venture Inn is your last chance to have a peaceful pint of beer before you arrive at the more hectic Casemates Square.

Once at Casemates you will be spoilt for choice with bars and pubs to suit all tastes, from the upmarket **Café Solo** to the more traditional **Lord Nelson**, which commemorates the life of one of Britain's great naval heroes. Also in Casemates, the **All's Well** pub has some interesting displays including a model of a whirlygig, an unusual contraption used to punish women of loose morals during the early years of British rule on the Rock. The pub's name commemorates the days when the city gates were locked at dusk and the duty sentry would shout "All's Well" before taking the keys to the governor's residence for safe keeping.

With the selection of pubs and late-night clubs in Casemates Square, there will surely be something to keep people of all tastes occupied well into the early hours of the morning.

– Walk 9 –
Gibraltar from the
Cruise Terminal

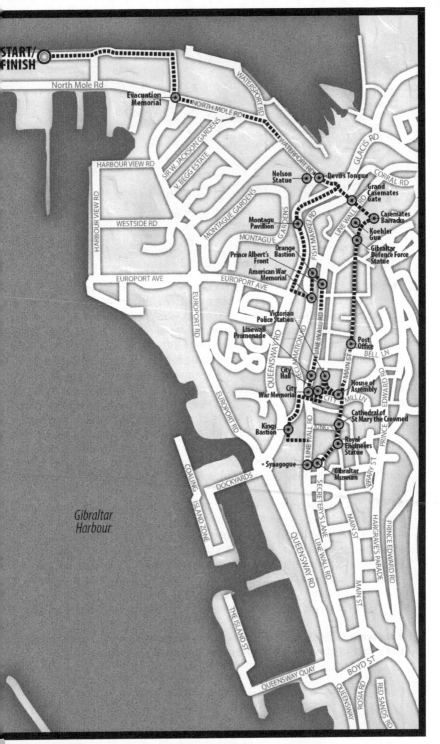

START/FINISH

North Mole Rd

Evacuation Memorial

NORTH MOLE RD

WATERSPORT RD

HARBOUR VIEW RD

SIR W. JACKSON GARDENS

V. BEGG ESTATE

GLACIS RD

CORRAL RD

HARBOUR VIEW RD

WESTSIDE RD

MONTAGUE GARDENS

MONTAGUE GARDENS

Nelson Statue

Devil's Tongue

Grand Casemates Gate

LINE WALL RD

Casemates Barracks

Koehler Gun

EUROPORT AVE

EUROPORT RD

EUROPORT AVE

Montagu Pavilion

MONTAGUE

Orange Bastion

Prince Albert's Front

American War Memorial

FISH MARKET RD

Gibraltar Defence Force Statue

Victorian Police Station

Linewall Promenade

QUEENSWAY RD

RECLAMATION RD

LINE WALL RD

MAIN ST

BELL LN

Post Office

City Hall

City War Memorial

House of Assembly

CITY

MILL LN

Cathedral of St Mary the Crowned

PRINCE EDWARD RD

Kings Bastion

LINE WALL RD

KINGS

Royal Engineers Statue

Synagogue

Gibraltar Museum

SECRETARY'S LANE

MAIN ST

LIBRARY ST

HARGRAVE'S PARADE

PRINCE EDWARD RD

EUROPORT RD

Gibraltar Harbour

COALING ISLAND ZONE

DOCKYARDS

THE ISLAND ST

QUEENSWAY RD

LINE WALL RD

SECRETARY'S LANE

MAIN ST

BOYD ST

ROSIA RD

RED SANDS RD

QUEENSWAY QUAY

QUEENSWAY

© Gibmetal77 / Wikimedia Commons

The Strait of Gibraltar has been a key Mediterranean trade route for centuries, with the Rock one of its most prominent attractions. It was a popular visiting point for the Phoenician merchants who plied their trade along these routes and regarded the Rock as having special religious significance. Phoenician artefacts dating from between 800 – 300 BC have been found in Gorham's cave which was thought to be shrine to the local protective spirit. Mariners crossing the Strait would have presumably visited this and other shrines on the Rock and asked the spirit to grant them safe passage through its turbulent waters. Gibraltar, known as Mons Calpe to the Romans, was considered by them to be one of the Pillars of Hercules, marking the westernmost limit of the known world. According to legend, Hercules was sent to fetch the Cattle of Geryon from the island of Erytheia as part of his Labours and split the Atlas mountains with his mace, joining as he did so the Atlantic Ocean with the Mediterranean Sea and forming the Rock of Gibraltar in the process.

Although it received many visitors throughout antiquity, there were no civilised settlements on the Rock until the Moorish arrived in the 8th Century AD. Gibraltar was held in such high regard that visiting the Rock was considered a great honour, such that according to the ancient Greek traveller Euctemon "to remain (in Gibraltar) was sacrilege". There has now been a permanent population on the Rock for over 1,300 years, with millions more visiting each year. Of these visitors, half a million arrive in Gibraltar like the Phoenicians did - by boat, disembarking for just a few hours at a time.

This walk is designed for passengers on board cruise liners to make the most of their short stay on the Rock.

Getting your bearings: This walk begins at the Cruise Terminal on the western end of the North Mole and follows a route both along and on the outside of the City walls. It then visits John Mackintosh Square, the King's Bastion (Gibraltar's most formidable defensive fortification) and the Gibraltar Museum before making a quick stop at Roman Catholic Cathedral of St. Mary the Crowned before returning to the Ferry Terminal via Main Street and Casemates Square.

Length: Approximately 3 km (3 hours +1 hour for the museum)

*Making your way out of the **cruise terminal**, follow the path of the North Mole eastwards in the direction of the Rock, passing the rather unsightly power station on your right hand side and the newly built Waterport Terraces housing estate on your left. After about 100 metres you will arrive at a roundabout containing a statue built to commemorate the evacuation of Gibraltarians during World War II. The **Evacuation Monument**, which is set in bronze and designed by British sculptor Jill Cowie Sanders and depicts a scene of evacuees being reunited with their family on return to the Rock. It was erected in November 2000 as a tribute to the thousands of civilians who were sent to Jamaica, Morocco, Madeira and the British Isles as Gibraltar prepared itself for attack by Germany and its allies. Many of the Gibraltarians who were evacuated to London lost their lives during the many German bombings of the city.*

*Continuing east for a further 100 or so metres, passing the coach terminal on your left hand side, you will arrive at a further roundabout which marks the eastern end of the area once known as the **Devil's Tongue**, now Waterport Wharf Road. The Devil's Tongue, known as such by the Spanish due to the damage which it was said to have inflicted on Spanish shipping in the Bay, was originally built as an extension of the Old Mole which itself had been rebuilt and extended many times since it was first constructed in a primitive form during the Merinid occupation of Gibraltar in the Fourteenth Century.*

The mole originally extended from **Chatham's Counterguard**, *which can be seen ahead of you in the distance and a drawbridge, which was known as the "Chatham Wicket", led from within the city walls to the mole. The original opening in the sea wall, now bricked-up, is still visible on Chatham Counterguard.*

The Devil's Tongue in its present form was built during the Great Siege and it was constructed with the intention of bringing flanking fire on the Spanish lines. However, on the recommendation of General Sir John Burgoyne, the inspector-general of fortifications who visited the Rock in 1848, the defences of the Devil's Tongue were turned around to provide south-facing protection to the harbour rather than remain pointed towards the isthmus where

they had proved to be relatively ineffective. It now has an extension on its western flank (the North Mole) which is about 1,600 feet long running in the direction of the Detached Mole as well as five additional jetties. These jetties were built during the early part of the last century as a Commercial Mole but were soon taken over by the Admiralty to accommodate destroyer flotillas, only being returned to the civilian authorities in the 1960's.

You will note on your right hand side as you make your way towards the Rock, a **statue of Admiral Sir George Rooke** who was the first British military governor of Gibraltar having commanded the allied naval forces during the capture of the Rock on 21 July, 1704. The statue was erected in 2004 to commemorate the tercentenary of this event. Passing the larger Waterport Roundabout and making your way through a road-sized gap in the counterguard, you will find yourself in Market Square, known colloquially as 'La Plaza del Reloj' due to the clock tower which has existed in the square at various locations and guises for many years. Adjacent to the Public Market, **Grand Case-**

mates Gate leads into Casemates Square where Gibraltar's medieval harbour once stood, built within the City's walls to protect it from fierce easterly and westerly winds and accessed via a small inlet which run through the Water Gate into the location of the present square. The original Water Gate was positioned just north of the present and the bricked-up arch of this gate was discernable until the line wall was reconstructed in Eighteenth Century.

Casemates Square is now the hub of the Rock's nightlife and leads on to Main Street which is Gibraltar's primary commercial thoroughfare. The remains of the medieval atarazana or galley-house can still be seen in a fenced enclosure outside of the Little Rock bar. This is the southern wall of, a roofed jetty about 40 metres in length where the medieval inhabitants of the town would have repaired their galleys or protected them during enemy attack or stormy weather. The Galley House was altered and used as a shot house during the early years of the British occupation before being damaged during the Great Siege and destroyed completely towards the end of the Eighteenth Century when the **Casemates Barracks**, located at the northern end of the Square were being built. Although some of the atarazana's foundations were excavated during the Square's recent renovation, the majority remain concealed below the Barracks. This Square is an excellent vantage point for admiring the **Moorish Castle** which overlooks the Square (for more information on the Moorish Castle and the remnants of Gibraltar's Moorish past, see *Walk 2, Moorish Gibraltar* on page 42).

Retracing your footsteps back to the Waterport roundabout, turn left and make your way along the outside of the Montagu Counterguard onto **Queensway**, formerly known as Reclamation Road but renamed after Queen Elizabeth II visited Gibraltar in 1954 as part of her Commonwealth Tour. It should be remembered that all land outside of the counterguard has been reclaimed from the sea over the last century, with large parts only having been reclaimed in the last 20 years. The **Montagu Pavilion** on your right as you follow the curve of the road was, as recently as the late 1980's, a bathing pavilion on the sea front, only recently having been converted into modern offices.

Follow the path along the outside of Chatham Counterguard and turn left until you find yourself at Prince Albert's Front and the **American War Memorial**. The archway and steps which blend into the original limestone coursed ashlar wall were commissioned by the American Battle Commission in 1932 to commemorate the co-operation of American and British Forces at Gibraltar during the First World War. There are two plaques mounted nearby, the first commemorates the arrival of the first American naval squadron to Gibraltar in 1801. The second, a more recent addition, commemorates Operation Torch, the Allied invasion of North Africa in November 1942, which was launched and commanded from Gibraltar.

Follow the so-called 'American Steps' onto **Line Wall Curtain**, which like so many other walls in Gibraltar was built roughly on the site of the original medieval sea wall. The actual Line Wall stretches beyond South Bastion up to Engineer Battery to the south of the town, however the road known nowadays as Line Wall is that which extends between the North and South bastions. On your left hand side as you come to the top of the steps you will see two 32-pounders on a south facing embrasure and a further two facing north on the right hand side of the bastion. You are standing on the former St Anne's Platform, now **Orange Bastion** which was named after William III of England who was Prince of Orange by birth. This curiously shaped bastion was, like Montagu Bastion, modernized in the late Nineteenth Century to encompass a heavy RML battery with iron shields. It mounted two 10-inch 18-ton RMLs during this time, and barrels have recently been restored to this position offering a nostalgic view of what the bastion might have looked like in Victorian times. From the bastion's left flank you can see a further four cannon on Chatham Counterguard facing south and west, these are a mix of 32 and 24 pounders on modern carriages which were placed here during a recent renovation of the City's defences.

Follow the short staircase onto **Prince Albert's Front** which lies parallel to Line Wall Road. This defensive wall runs between Orange Bastion and King's Bastion and is the site of a former saluting battery. Prince Albert's Front, named after Queen Victoria's husband, the Prince Consort, was restored for use as a car parking area and has been built on quite extensively, including community centre built at the far end of the wall on Zoca Flank Battery. The word 'Zoca' is thought to have derived from the Arabic word zoco or souq which referred to the market which would have stood in close proximity. This battery is in general disrepair, being mainly used to alleviate Gibraltar's car parking problems.

However, on this stretch of the line wall you will come across an 18th century expense magazine and various sets of small steps (known as banquettes) which allowed the protecting forces to fire over the crest of the parapet.

Descend the steps from Prince Albert's Front onto Line Wall Promenade, an area which was cut from the city walls in 1921 during the Governorship of General Sir Horace Smith-Dorrien. Immediately on your right hand side at the base of the steps is a small disused fountain set into the wall of the bastion. This fountain which was supplied by an aqueduct was built in 1571 and was originally situated in the Piazza adjacent to the building which is now the **City Hall** (near 'Fountain Ramp' which took its name). The fountain was moved to Castle Street at the end of the Nineteenth Century and continued to be in use until it was moved to its present location in 1967. In the centre of the Promenade is the City War Memorial which was erected in 1923 by public subscription at the not insignificant cost at the time of £1,700. This memorial was sculpted from Carrara marble by Catalan Sculptor Jose Piquet Catoli and commemorates those Gibraltarians who died during the First World War. The memorial and steps are flanked on either side by Russian Guns 24 Pounder cannons which had been captured by the British during the Crimean War and given as a gift to the people of Gibraltar. Kings Bastion lies at the southern end of the Promenade, and a plaque at the far end commemorates the life of General Sir Robert Boyd, a former Governor of Gibraltar who helped design the King's Bastion and whose body is interred in a special chamber built within the bastion walls. Before exploring one of Gibraltar's most impressive defensive fortifications, make your way back to the City War Memorial and cross the road in the direction of John Macintosh Square, known nowadays as the **Piazza**. This Square has undergone various refurbishments and name changes throughout the years but few will deny its importance as one of the most prominent squares and meeting places for Gibraltarians. The Piazza used to be called Commercial Square and during this time hosted a daily flea market and public auctions, inspiring its other colloquial nickname 'el Martillo' meaning literally 'the hammer'. In 1940 the Square's name was changed once again to honour the memory of local philanthropist John Mackintosh whose bust overlooks the square.

The square is flanked on either side by two of Gibraltar's most important buildings. The **House of Assembly**, the front of which overlooks Main Street was built in 1817 as the Exchange and Commercial Library by then Governor Sir George Don, whose own bust can be seen on the upper part of the building from Main Street. The building was funded by public subscription and a list of the subscribers can still be seen in the building's lobby. After becoming Gibraltar's Commercial Library, the building was damaged by fire in 1919 and large parts of it were re-built in a different style to the original building. In

1950 the building became Gibraltar's Legislative Council and then in 1969, it became the House of Assembly which was Gibraltar's equivalent to the Houses of Parliament. In 2006 it was finally renamed the Gibraltar Parliament.

Opposite the House of Assembly is the building known today as the **City Hall**. This building was built in 1819 as a private mansion for Aaron Nunez Cardozo, a wealthy Jewish merchant who settled in Gibraltar. After Cardozo died in 1834 the building's use changed several times including its time as the exclusive Club House Hotel. It was also temporarily the residence of the Duke of Connaught, Queen Victoria's son, who was stationed in Gibraltar in the early 1900's and began to be known as Connaught House. The building was eventually sold to the Gibraltar Government in 1920 for around £40,000 and became the offices of the newly formed City Council, adopting its current name. A plaque on the exterior of the building details its recent history (further information on the City Hall and in particular its links to Admiral Nelson are described in *Walk 4, Naval Gibraltar* on page 78).

Before returning to Line Wall Promenade to continue the walk, it is also worth noting the **Victorian police station** on Irish Town at the northern end of the Square. This building was constructed in 1864 during the governorship of General Sir William Codrington and was the main headquarters of the Royal Gibraltar Police until this was relocated to the police station at New Mole House. Back at the Promenade, follow the steps down to Reclamation Road which leads to the entry to Kings Bastion itself. **Kings Bastion** is perhaps the grandest of all of Gibraltar's fortifications and, built on the site of the former Platform of Saint Lawrence its location was key in the protection of the City, standing as it does in the foreground of the **Cathedral of St. Mary the**

Crowned. Although the idea of a bastion on this site was originally proposed by Colonel Skinner in 1758, it was Chief Engineer William Green who designed the bastion in 1773 with the assistance of the aforementioned Boyd.

The Bastion, with its parapets of solid masonry up to 15-feet thick and a not significant armament of twelve **32-pounders** and ten 10-inch howitzers just on its front, was General Eliott's command post during the Great Siege. There are various displays about the bastion's history on the entry tunnel and many of the original building plans are on show at the 'internet zone' at the southern end of the Bastion. You will also be able to see arched cooking areas at the interior of the entry tunnel, with carved ducts to carry away the fumes. The armoured casemates on the top floor of the Bastion which once housed heavy duty weaponry now house a wine bar and disco (for more information on the guns mounted on the Kings Bastion, see *Walk 5, The Guns of Gibraltar* on Page 94).

The bastion was decommissioned in the early 1900s and soon fell into neglect with the internal areas being used by the Public Works Department and a generating station built onto its northern side in the 1960's. The generating station was demolished in 2005 revealing the bastion's attractive façade for the first time in almost half a century. Kings Bastion took on a new lease of life in 2007 when the building was elegantly renovated making way for a bowling alley, ice-skating rink as well as a multi-screen cinema and other leisure facilities. A particular quality of the Leisure Centre is the tasteful way in which many aspects of the bastion's original character have been restored to their original glory. In particular the casemated gun emplacements on the roof with guns flanking to the Bastion's left and right side are worthy of a visit, giving a very good impression of what the Bastion would have looked like in the late Eighteenth Century. The defences were improved at the end of the Nineteenth Century and armoured casemates were added. The barrels of the 12.5-inch 38-ton and the four 10-inch 18-ton RMLs guns which guard the front

of the Bastion give some indication of the firing power this Bastion would have had at that time.

After exiting Kings Bastion, return to Line Wall Promenade and skirt the eastern edge of the bastion along Line Wall Road until you see the **Great Synagogue of Gibraltar***. This was the first synagogue to operate on the Iberian Peninsula after the expulsion of the Jews from Spain in 1492. It was founded in 1724 by Isaac Nieto on a plot of land granted to the Jews of Gibraltar by then Governor Brigadier General Richard Kane although much of the present structure was built in the early Nineteenth Century. Next to the Great Synagogue is the* **Gibraltar Museum** *which houses some of the most important objects relating to Gibraltar's history ranging from Palaeolithic and Bronze Age artefacts to 20th Century prints and photographs. The museum was officially opened in 1930 by then Governor General Sir Alexander Godley and the building had previously been home of Gibraltar's Principal Ordinance Officer. The patio, which can be accessed free of charge, features the archaeological remains of a 16th Century Spanish Aqueduct which carried water to a cistern within the museum building as well as some earlier Muslim structures.*

Entry to the museum is highly recommended, particularly considering its low admission price of only £2.00 for adults. A short video is played near the museum's entrance giving an excellent précis on Gibraltar's history in under 15 minutes. You can run through the museum in about an hour, however you will probably need at least two to make the most of the museum's full collection. The exhibitions do not always follow a chronological theme, giving the museum a slightly haphazard feel at times as you jump forward and back through different periods of Gibraltar's history. Particularly worthy of mention is the scale model of the Rock which provides a thoroughly detailed three-dimensional view of Gibraltar as it was during

© Bjørn, via Flickr

the late 19th Century. The model was one of two built in 1868 by Sappers Williams and McLellan from a survey made by Lieutenant Charles Warren of the Royal Engineers who also oversaw the model's completion. The complex of medieval baths situated in the basement of the building are undoubtedly the jewel in the Museum's crown and represent one of the most complete examples of baths of this type that can be found in Europe today (these are described in more detail in Walk 2 on Moorish Gibraltar on page ##).

The Gibraltar Museum
18/20 Bomb House Lane
Gibraltar
Tel: +350 200 74298
Fax: +350 200 79158
Email: enquiries@museum.gib.gi
Open: Monday to Friday 10:00 – 18:00 (last entry at 17:30), Saturday 10:00 to 14:00 (last entry at 13:30) Sundays: Closed
Admission: Adults: £2.00, Children (aged 12 and under): £1.00, Under 5's: free.

Turn left as you exit the museum and head up Bomb House Lane, past the **Deanery** - the official residence of the Dean of Gibraltar until you reach Main Street. The first thing you will see is a plinth with a life-size statue commemorating the Royal Engineers and their services to Gibraltar. Though military engineers have always served in the armies of the Crown, the origins of the modern corps of Royal Engineers have their roots in the Soldier Artificer Company established for service in Gibraltar in 1782 as the first non-commissioned military engineers. The Royal Engineers in their various forms are responsible for many of Gibraltar's fortifications with their most noteworthy legacy being the labyrinthine network of tunnels through the Rock and which have had such a pivotal role in Gibraltar's defence through the years. The tunnels were an amazing feat of engineering and were described by the Duc de Crillon, who commanded the defeated French and Spanish attackers at the Great Siege, as being: "worthy of the Romans".

*Across the road you will see the **Cathedral of St Mary the Crowned** which was built on the site of what was, during the Muslim occupation of the Rock, Gibraltar's main mosque. When Gibraltar came under Spanish rule, Queen Isabella ordered that it be rebuilt as a church in a Gothic style, with a typical high dock and bell tower. The structure survived the British conquest but suffered extensive damage during frequent attacks and particularly during the Great Siege. It was once again rebuilt in 1790 during Sir Robert Boyd's second tenure as the Governor of Gibraltar. It was at this time that its main façade was repositioned to where it is today in an effort to straighten Main Street.*

Although remnants of the Spanish structure still remain, numerous refurbishments have meant that the Cathedral as it stands today differs greatly from that which was built under Queen Isabella's rule. Entering the Cathedral via the side entrance (to the left of the Cathedral's main entrance), you find yourself in what remains of the courtyard once known as the Patio de los Naranjos (Courtyard of the Orange Trees). Set into the wall on the court's eastern wall you can still make out the coat-of-arms of Queen Isabella and King Ferdinand of Spain. The patio also leads to the Chapel of Our Lady of Lourdes and the archway which forms the entrance to the chapel was part of the original Spanish church, giving some indication of the church's original height and shape. The interior of the chapel was built in the late 19th century by then Bishop, Gonzalo Canilla and his Episcopal seal adorns the front of the altar.

Entering the Cathedral's main building via the side door, you will be immediately drawn to the spectacularly high Italian marble altar which was said to have been built in a style similar to the altar of St Peter's Basilica in Rome. It had originally been constructed for use in a church in South America, but when the ship carrying it sank in the Bay of Gibraltar, the altar was salvaged and donated to the Cathedral. There are statues of the Four Evangelists on the altar and relics of the saints dating back to the Spanish period can be found at the base of each statue. To the left of the high altar is the altar of St Mary the Crowned which is adorned with a statue of St Mary. The original statue which gave the church its name can only be viewed by private appointment as it is located within the Church's sacristy. There are various memorial tablets on the floor of the sanctuary and throughout the church. On the right hand side of the High Altar, in front of the Altar of the Blessed Sacrament a memorial honours Monsignor Narciso Pallares, a member of the local clergy who was murdered in the Cathedral by a madman in 1885. The Cathedral's stained glass windows are mainly modern having been replaced when the RFA Bedenham, a naval armament carrier, exploded while docked in Gibraltar in 1951, shattering many of the original windows.

Cathedral of Saint Mary the Crowned

215 Main Street
Tel: +350 200 76688
Fax: +350 200 43112
Email: cathedral@gibtelecom.net
Mass held: Monday to Friday – 07:30, 09:15, 12:25 & 18:15
*   Saturday – 18:30 (family mass)*
*   Sunday – 09:00, 10:30, 12:00 & 18:30*

Exiting the Cathedral from its main entrance, you can either turn right to head back to the start of the walk or, time permitting, turn left and continue your path up Main Street towards Gibraltar's Church of England Cathedral, the Cathedral of the Holy Trinity (If so, join *Walk 3, North to South* on Page 54 continuing the route from the Cathedral of the Holy Trinity up to the Alameda Gardens which will add approximately 1.5 hours more to the walk).

Heading north in the direction of Casemates Square you will note that at first observation Main Street appear to mirror the style of many typical British pedestrian shopping avenues and indeed the many Georgian constructions along its length verify this contention. However looking above street level, the elaborate wrought-iron balconies and the many tiled façades paint a vastly different picture, as do the wooden shutters which adorn almost every window. You will soon see Gibraltar's main **Post Office** on your left hand side. The post office was established in Gibraltar in 1857, when the Overland Post Office and the Packet Agency were merged under the control of Britain's Postmaster General. Plans were soon adopted to build a new post office building and on 1 September 1858 the Gibraltar Post Office at 104 Main Street was inaugurated, just a few months after British postage stamps were first placed on sale in Gibraltar.

A set of red telephone boxes mark the beginning southern most edge of **Casemates Square** off Main Street. Across the road, by the taxi rank there is a statue of a **Soldier of the Gibraltar Defence Force** (GDF). The GDF paraded for the first time on the 28th of April, 1939 and is a forerunner of what is now the Royal Gibraltar Regiment. Composed of local volunteers, the GDF served side-by-side with the regular units of the Garrison and this statue symbolises Gibraltar's role in the defence of the Rock during the Second World War.

Another feature of the square is a replica of the so-called Koehler Gun positioned on a plinth in front of the **Tourist Office**. *The gun, incorporating*

a design developed in Gibraltar during the Great Siege (1779-1783) is distinctive for its downwards facing barrel which allowed it to be placed on an embrasure or rocky promontory with a steep angle of depression and be pointed directly on the besieging enemy. The design of this gun has been attributed to Lieutenant George

Koehler who served in Gibraltar during the Great Siege. It was first tested in 1782 and was based on a normal wooden garrison carriage which was split horizontally down its centre with a hinge at the front to adjust the trajectory. Unlike other contemporary guns, the barrel was attached to a sliding timber plank which dealt with the recoil.

Make your way to Casemates Barracks which dominate the northern end of the square and lie parallel to Grand Battery. These were originally designed in 1770 by Chief Engineer William Green as bombproof accommodation for soldiers but were not completed until 1817. Despite its renovation in the mid-1990s, these former barracks retain many of the building's original features. They are now a large arcade with bars and restaurants, niche boutiques and an art gallery, giving you a final chance to pick up some Gibraltar souvenirs before exiting the old city via **Waterport Gate** and following the route via Waterport Wharf Road back to the Cruise Terminal.

– Useful Information –

Where to Stay

Accommodation in Gibraltar tends to be on the expensive side. Hotels have struggled to keep up with the burgeoning tourist trade and while there are various hotel projects being planned for the near future, hotel rooms are in fairly limited supply at the moment. Therefore it is worth booking your accommodation well in advance of travelling to Gibraltar, particularly during peak seasons such as summer and traditional UK holidays.

Key (Room prices are per night and based on a double room with breakfast included.)

£   - less than £50

££   - £50 - £100

£££   - more than £100

The O'Callaghan Eliott Hotel - £££

The Eliott Hotel sets the standard as far as modernity goes. Situated in the heart of Gibraltar's business and shopping districts, just off Main Street, this recently refurbished city hotel is the obvious choice for the business traveller. Guests can enjoy the swimming pool facilities on the roof of the hotel as well as spacious rooms with balconies. The hotel offers an excellent buffet breakfast and the Rooftop Restaurant offers guests and non-guests the opportunity to enjoy classic continental cuisine with magnificent views over the Bay of Gibraltar. The Veranda Bar offers a lighter dining alternative and is also worth a mention for its lively jazz sessions every Thursday night.

The O'Callaghan Eliott Hotel
Governor's Parade
Gibraltar
Tel. +350 200 70500
Fax +350 200 70243
www.ocallaghanhotels.com/eliott

The Rock Hotel - £££

Built by the Marquis of Bute in 1932, the Rock Hotel is the epitome of British colonial charm. With a guestbook that boasts the signatures of Winston

Churchill and Errol Flynn it is hardly surprising that it has long been considered the most luxurious place to stay in Gibraltar. This sentiment is mirrored by the AA who rate it higher than any other hotel on the Rock and the RAC who have awarded it a white ribbon and two dining awards. Guest rooms are light and airy and most have balconies with excellent views over the Bay of Gibraltar. In addition rooms come with all the added extras you would expect from so grand a hotel, from bathrobes and a trouser press to rubber ducks in the bathrooms. The hotel also has an excellent pool area on the edge of the Alameda Botanical gardens. While the hotel is situated outside of the town area, Main Street is only a five-minute walk away and a regular bus service stops right outside the hotel.

The Rock Hotel
3 Europa Road
Gibraltar
Tel. +350 200 73000
Fax +350 200 73513
rockhotel@gibtelecom.net
www.rockhotelgibraltar.com

The Caleta Hotel - £££

Positioned on a rocky outcrop overlooking Catalan Bay, a traditional fishing village and cove that share the same name, this hotel is the perfect choice for visitors wishing to avoid the hustle and bustle of the city centre. This hotel is particularly well placed during the warm season (May-September, give or take a few weeks) to enjoy Gibraltar's vibrant beach life. The pool area, with its path leading down to the beach, is adequate though it must be said, perhaps slightly outmoded. While offering excellent access to most of Gibraltar's beaches, the hotel is arguably too far from Main Street to be considered walking distance, so you are left to rely on the bus service and taxis. The hotel boasts a lovely lounge and bar area as well as two quality restaurants, with one of them (Nuno's) recently awarded two AA rosettes. A word of warning, guests at this hotel should make sure they secure their windows when leaving the room or they may be treated to an unwanted visit from cheeky Barbary macaques.

The Caleta Hotel
Sir Herbert Miles Road
Gibraltar

Tel. +350 200 76501
reservations@caletahotel.gi
www.caletahotel.com

The Bristol Hotel - ££

Set in the heart of town, the Bristol Hotel offers guests the opportunity of being literally a stone's throw from Main Street while still being able to enjoy the relaxing luxury of a swimming pool. Not as expensive as the "big three", the Bristol is decorated in an albeit outdated, British colonial style starting with its bleach-white exterior. Being so close to the centre of town has its downsides though and the rooms might be a tad noisy in the evenings, however this is pretty much the case in most places in Gibraltar. There is also a reasonably priced snack bar that claims to offer the cheapest drinks in town.

The Bristol Hotel
8/10 Cathedral Square
Gibraltar
Tel. +350 200 76800
Fax +350 200 77613
reservations@bristolhotel.gi
www.bristolhotel.gi

Queen's Hotel - ££

The Queen's is situated near Charles V Wall on the southern end of Main Street. Though it is located close to the Rock Hotel, it might as well be a million miles away considering the gulf in quality. This is not to say that the Queen's Hotel is not worth every penny of its fairly low room price. The décor throughout the hotel is old fashioned but the rooms are clean and the staff polite and attentive. The Queens is certainly an option for the budget traveller and although the rooms are basic they do offer en suite bathrooms, satellite TV in all the rooms and a fairly decent cooked breakfast in the morning. The hotel offers free parking and is positioned close to the Cable Car and the Alameda Botanical Gardens.

Queen's Hotel
1 Boyd Street
Gibraltar

Tel. +350 200 74000
Fax +350 200 40030
queenshotel@gibtelecom.net
www.queenshotel.gi

Cannon Hotel - £/££

The Cannon Hotel is unquestionably the choice for the budget traveller. It is perfectly positioned in the heart of town giving unrivalled access to the bustling Main Street area. Room prices are relatively inexpensive by Gibraltar's standards and this includes a decent cooked breakfast. Unfortunately not all rooms are en suite and communal bathroom facilities are of hostel standard to say the least. Rooms are generally clean but extremely basic and crucially lacking in air conditioning. The hotel can also be noisy at times as noises from the exterior as well as from the inner courtyard tend to resonate through the rooms of the hotel.

The Cannon Hotel
9 Cannon Lane
Gibraltar
Tel. +350 200 51711
Fax +350 200 51789
cannon@gibnet.gi
www.cannonhotel.gi

Governor's Inn Apartments - £/££

Situated on Governors Street in the heart of the old town area, you are right in the middle of Gibraltar's hustle and bustle. These apartments sleep up to five people, so are the perfect low-cost option for travelling groups. All apartments have cable TV as well as fully-fitted kitchens with pots, pans, cutlery and all the mod-cons, including a washing machine. There is also an attached office downstairs with telephones, internet access and photocopying.

Governor's Inn Apartments
36 Governors Street
Gibraltar
Tel. +350 200 44227
Fax +350 200 79992

gibc@gibraltar.gi
www.gibc.gi

Ocean Heights Apartments - £/££

These apartments situated within a popular residential block offer basic amenities at low prices. They are located centrally and boast a slightly dated swimming pool all year round. Again, this is the perfect option for those travelling in larger groups or anyone preferring the luxuries a self-catering apartment can offer. Apartments are available either through:

Herald Travel
Suite 11
Ocean Heights
Gibraltar
Tel. +350 200 71250
lettings@heraldproperties.net
www.heraldproperties.net

or

Jade Travel
Ocean Heights.
Gibraltar
Tel. +350 56585000
info@gibraltarholidays.com
www.gibraltarholidays.com

Emile Youth Hostel - £

Gibraltar's only youth hostel offers basic accommodation either on a private room or dormitory basis for about £10-15 a night depending on the time of year. It is well situated overlooking Casemates Square and is the perfect choice for backpackers or young travellers. The rooms are clean and even the communal areas are kept spotless at all times. While it is largely meant for young people, it is unlikely that anyone will be turned away if they have spare rooms. The youth hostel is often booked out for portions of the year to accommodate youth exchanges from abroad.

Emile Youth Hostel
Montagu Bastion
Line Wall Road
Gibraltar
Tel. +350 200 51106
emilehostel@yahoo.co.uk

Where to Eat

Gibraltarians are a fusion of the European immigrants who arrived at the Rock from Italy, Spain, Malta and India at various times throughout Gibraltar's history. When you add Gibraltar's Jewish community, the influence of nearby Morocco and over 300 years of British rule, you are left with a truly multi-layered society. The melting-pot of cultures and backgrounds together with the unique circumstances to which Gibraltar has been subjected have resulted in a truly unique people and unsurprisingly diverse culinary practices.

There are a wide and varied range of cafes and restaurants to suit all budgets and literally all tastes are catered for. It is very common for people to order raciones or "portions", which are placed at the centre of the table for everyone to share. Order a few different plates at first and if you are hungry later, order more, no one is waiting for your table.

£   - less than £15
££   - £15 - £25
£££ - £25 - £35
Prices are based on a per person basis including drinks.

Morocco Restaurant - £

A truly authentic Moroccan restaurant that has been offering quality North African cuisine from its location on Turnbull's Lane since the 1970s. Its tiny interior can only accommodate a few tables, so it is best to visit during the warmer months when al fresco dining is a more reasonable option. The beef and chicken pinchitos (meat skewers) are arguably the best on the Rock.

Morocco Restaurant
46 Turnbulls Lane
Gibraltar
Tel. +350 200 70859

Jumpers - £

Jumpers is probably Gibraltar's most popular Fish restaurant. Located on North Jumpers Bastion this restaurant is particularly favoured by hard-to-please local diners. The food is top notch and inexpensive offering a wide range of seafood as well as meat dishes on a raciones basis. Best to book in advance during the summer, which is the fresh fish season.

Jumpers Wheel Restaurant

Jumpers Bastion
Rosia Road
Tel. +350 200 40052

Marrakech Restaurant - £

Situated on a quiet square by the Eliott Hotel, Marrakech is a slightly more upmarket option than Morocco Restaurant for visitors wishing to taste authentic Moroccan cuisine on the Rock. Al fresco dining in the summer is complimented by a homely and charmingly decorated interior. An opportunity to savour some great Moroccan cuisine including lamb tagine and couscous, pastilla (meat pie) and traditional Moroccan soup known as harira.

Marrakech Restaurant

7 Governors Parade
Gibraltar
Tel. +350 200 75196

Maharaja - £

The original and possibly the best curry house on the Rock. Positioned just off Main Street, near Barclay's Bank, the Maharaja offers un-extravagant and economically priced Indian food with a fully stocked bar, making it the perfect place to begin your night out. The Maharaja franchise has now extended and there is a slightly more up-market Maharaja on the Queensway Quay marina.

Maharaja

5 Tuckey's LaneGibraltar
Tel. +350 200 75233

Maharaja

17B Ragged Staff Wharf
Queensway Quay
Gibraltar
Tel. +350 200 50733

El Capote - £/££

Charming little tapas bar very much in the Andalusian style. Located on Market Lane between Main Street and Irish Town, El Capote, meaning literally "the Cloak" has been doing a great job emulating the style of La Línea's popular tapas bars. There are a selection of hot dishes on the menu, such as huevos a la Flamenca, a very typical regional dish made with Spanish ham and fried eggs as well as montaditos (pork loin sandwiches) and pinchitos (meat skewers). It is also a good place to sample cold cuts of Iberian meats and cheeses. Order by the portion, or merely individual tapas and accompany with a fino sherry or a glass of Rioja wine. The restaurant only opens for lunch except on Fridays when the bar remains open until around midnight.

El Capote
13 Market Lane
Gibraltar
Tel. +350 200 75222

Biancas - ££

The ever-popular Biancas is situated within the Marina Bay complex and offers the best in quayside eating. It is very much a Gibraltar standard and tends to get very busy during peak times, even despite its spacious interior. A varied international menu offers something for every taste but it is the desserts that steal the show, particularly the great selection of ice-cream sundaes. The bar area also offers a very reasonably priced snack menu and a wide selection of alcoholic as well as non-alcoholic beverages. Table reservations essential at weekends.

Biancas Restaurant
6-7 Admiral's Walk
Marina Bay
Gibraltar
Tel. +350 200 73379
Fax +350 200 79061

Café Rojo - ££

Situated on Irish Town this small restaurant is a popular choice for business lunches. The menu is impeccable with a great selection of pasta dishes and salads served in understated but modern surroundings. Be sure to book in advance at lunchtimes and weekends. Café Rojo also serves an excellent cup of coffee.

Café Rojo
54 Irish Town
Gibraltar
Tel. +350 200 51738

Charlie's Tavern - ££

Stock in Charlie's Steakhouse and Grill has truly risen in recent years, making it one of the go-to restaurant for locals seeking high-quality cuisine and a varied menu on the waterfront. As the name suggests, steaks and other grilled meats are readily available, as are an excellent selection of eastern food including Tandoori dishes, offered as part of their 'Passage to India' menu. Along with Bianca's next door, this restaurant can be extremely busy on weekends, particularly Sunday lunchtime, so its well worth booking ahead. There is also a pleasant bar area which has become a popular place to watch live sport accompanied by a pint of beer and bar snacks.

Charlies Tavern
4/5 Britannia House
Marina Bay
Gibraltar
Bar tel. +350 200 79993
Restaurant tel. +350 200 69993
www.charliestavern.com

4 Stagioni - ££

Located in an old expense magazine built in the 18th century, this restaurant on the Saluting Battery (near Jumpers Bastion), offers some of the best pizza and pasta dishes you will find on the Rock and at affordable prices. This is a perfect family restaurant and a substantial menu also caters for younger diners.

4 Stagioni
Rosia Road

Jumpers Bastion
Gibraltar
Tel/Fax +350 200 79153
4stagioni@gibtelecom.net

Piccadilly Garden - ££

This restaurant, situated at the northern end of the Saluting Parade ("la ba-teria") on Rosia Road, has been offering great homemade fare to the local population for decades. There is a varied menu including tapas, fried fish and other raciones as well as a full a la carte menu. This restaurant is a popular venue to enjoy a traditional breakfast of churros (fried-dough snacks) on its spacious terrace. The restaurant is closed Sundays.

Picadilly Garden
3B Rosia Road
Gibraltar
Tel. +350 200 75758
picbar@hotmail.com

Casa Pepe - £££

Spanish cuisine with a few added surprises. Casa Pepe serves the best An-dalusian dishes from the quintessentially British surroundings of the Queen-sway Quay marina. A good place to sample the best jamón ibérico (Iberian cured ham) money can buy, and the jamón cooked with artichoke hearts is pure gastronomic delight.

Casa Pepe
Unit 18
Queensway Quay
Gibraltar
Tel. +350 200 46967

La Mamela - £££

Situated at the entrance to Catalan Bay, La Mamela is great for seafood lov-ers, serving fresh fish in beautiful surroundings overlooking the beach below.

It is the perfect place for a romantic candlelit dinner and their paellas are second to none on the Rock.

La Mamela
Catalan Bay
Sir Herbert Miles Road
Gibraltar
Tel. +350 200 72373

The Waterfront - £££

This popular restaurant is situated on the Queensway Quays waterfront over-looking the marina. It is tastefully decorated and a large conservatory area is ideal for dining during the warmer months of the year. The menu is extensive and varied including many Indian and Chinese dishes. Although the restaurant is perhaps slightly overpriced, their Sunday roast is about as good as you can get on the Rock and well worth the cost.

The Waterfront Restaurant
Queensway Quay Marina
Tel. +350 200 45666
Fax +350 200 45665
www.gibwaterfront.com

The Yellowhouse Restaurant - £££

The Yellow House Restaurant offers the finest in Andalusian haute cuisine in a handy City Centre location. This restaurant, located in a reformed colonial-style building on Parliament Lane is clearly one of the stars of the local restaurant scene. This Spanish-run restaurant boasts excellent service and a great selection of southern-influenced dishes of the highest calibre. The Iberian ham is amongst the best you can find locally and the ham canapes are a must-have. A great place for a steak and also arguably the best Caesar Salad in Gibraltar!

The YellowHouse Restaurant
Parliament Lane
Gibraltar
Tel. +350 200 48148 / +350 200 48248
www.yhrestaurant.com

Gaucho's - £££

Argentinean restaurant offering arguably the best steak on the Rock. Situated literally inside the City walls at Chatham Counterguard, the interior is tastefully decorated and distinguishes itself through its superb selection of meat dishes, cooked mainly on a large stone grill. The maître d' and highly attentive staff will do their best to make you feel at home and the recently opened outdoor area promises an alternative tapas menu that can be enjoyed al fresco day or night.

Gaucho's Restaurant
1 Fish Market Road
Tel. +350 200 59700

ORIENTAL

Kowloon - £/££

Decent mid-priced Chinese restaurant that has been a favourite with locals for decades. Also does takeaway.

Kowloon Restaurant
20 Watergardens 3
Waterport Road
Tel. +350 200 42771

Lek Bangkok - ££

The only restaurant selling authentic Thai cuisine on the Rock. Lek meticulously slaves over each dish and uses only the freshest ingredients to produce mouth watering Thai food. There is not a great deal of variety in its slightly limited menu, but most of the standard Thai dishes are cooked to the highest measure. Lek Bangkok has a fully stocked bar and its outside seating area is extremely popular during the warmer months.

Lek Bangkok
Unit 501/3 Block 5, Eurotowers
Tel. +350 200 48881

CAFES AND SNACK BARS

Sacarello's Coffee Shop - £

One of Gibraltar's most popular meeting spots, Sacarello's is primarily a coffee shop but also specializes in light lunches and snacks. It is the perfect place to enjoy a cup of coffee in the afternoon, accompanied by a cake or pastry. There is also a gift shop at the front selling luxury foods and their own special blends of coffee. Sacarello's closes Monday to Friday at 19:30 and 15:00 on Saturday. Closed on Sunday.

Sacarello's
Corner of Irish Town/Tuckey's Lane
Tel. +350 200 70625

Time Out Café - £

Situated in the Europort area near Morissons, Time Out Café is a popular destination for those seeking a light lunch or snack. The service is good and the food is of a decent quality and very reasonably priced.

Time Out Cafe
106 Eurotowers
Tel. +350 200 76044
Fax +350 200 72760

The Piazza Café Restaurant - £

Positioned at the heart of Main Street, outside the House of Assembly, there is no better place than the Piazza café to sit to watch the world go by. There is a varied and reasonably good value menu but the location is the main selling point.

The Piazza Café Restaurant
156/3 Main Street, Gibraltar
Tel. +350 200 47780
E-mail piazza@gibtelecom.net

Munchies Café - £

Good position at the northern end of Main Street near Casemates Square. Pre-packed sandwiches and soups for people on the go.

Munchies Café
24 Main Street
Gibraltar
Tel. +350 200 43840
Fax +350 200 42390

Amar's Bakery - £

Baker's, confectioner's, convenience store and cafeteria all rolled into one. Those Gibraltarian favourites Calentita and spinach pie are always on the menu and it is all kosher too!

Amar's Bakery
1A Convent Place
Gibraltar
Tel. +350 200 73516
Fax +350 200 76914

FAST FOOD

Gibraltar has not been immune to the unrelenting spread of global fast food brands. Over the last few years McDonalds, Burger King, KFC and Subway have all made their way to Gibraltar.

However small independent takeaways still rule the roost with the local population and the combination of Mediterranean with North African cuisine makes these establishments some of the best places to sample great local food.

Al Madina - £

With its enormously varied menu, there is definitely something for all tastes in this popular takeaway in Ocean Heights. Burgers, roast chicken, shish kebabs and chicken tikka are all on the menu, as are local delicacies such as stuffed courgettes or sardines, perfectly prepared by the ever-smiling chefs. There is also a fairly large eat-in area and occasionally traditional Moroccan cakes can be purchased here.

Al Madina
11/12 Ocean Heights Gallery
Queensway
Gibraltar
Tel. +350 200 46363

Gilbert's - £

Set into the West Place of Arms, near the public market, Gilbert's is definitely a Gibraltar institution. This takeaway is only open in the evenings where Gilbert himself serves up arguably some of the best fast food on the Rock. Steak rolls are one of the most popular items on the menu, enjoyed either with a fried egg or just alioli (garlic sauce) or mojo picón (spicy sauce). The pinchitos are top class and in particular their pollo adobo pinchito, a chicken skewer marinated in vinegar before it is cooked.

Gilbert's Takeaway
3 West Place of Arms
Gibraltar
Tel. +350 200 77582

Al Baraka - £

Its covered outdoor area is the perfect place to enjoy the varied menu on offer in this takeaway located in Queensway Quay, just a very short walk from the marina. This takeaway serves inexpensive kebabs, pinchitos and fried fish all to a decent standard.

Al Baraka
Unit 1 Queensway Quay
Gibraltar
Tel. +350 200 46993

Shopping

Gibraltar's Main Street provides a complete shopping experience to the millions who visit the Rock each year. It runs the entire length of the old city from Casemates Square to Charles V Wall and together with its many tributaries encompasses practically most of Gibraltar's commercial district.

Off-licences offering cheap cigarettes and alcohol to day-trippers will stand out initially but Gibraltar has much more to offer shoppers. For example perfumes and cosmetics are also available at extremely reasonable prices at many of the established perfumeries on Main Street. Many popular British high street brand names can also be found along Main Street's length—Marks and Spencer, Monsoon, Next, BHS and Top Shop to name but a few. There is also a Morrisons supermarket that is open seven days a week, packed to the brim with locals or foreign ex-pats who visit from the Costa del Sol.

Gibraltar's high street also offers a fairly large number of jewellers, electronics shops and shops selling crystal and porcelain goods. Many of these shops are run by Hindus of Indian descent whose families came to Gibraltar after the opening of the Suez Canal in 1869 to set up businesses on the Rock. They once ran bazaars selling everything under the sun but nowadays tend to specialize in luxury goods, which have been in high demand as a result of Gibraltar's booming economy.

Although many of the goods on sale are cheaper than on the UK high street, there is no harm in trying to haggle down the price a little more. While Ocean Village does its best to set the standard as far as high-end fashion is concerned, there is also an increasing number of designer clothes boutiques opening in the Main Street area. The Bang & Olufsen store sells high-end audio and visual products and there are specialist cigar shops and off licences that sell luxury consumables of this nature.

Tucked away down Gibraltar's side streets are several smaller independent shops offering bespoke crafts, jewellery and other specialist goods. In the Gibraltar Crystal shop on Casemates Square distinctive glass artwork is handcrafted before your very eyes, using cutting-edge designs. Also situated nearby is the Casemates Fine Arts Gallery which, like the Gibraltar Art Gallery on Cannon Lane, showcases for sale artwork produced by local artists.

Shops in Gibraltar tend to open from about 10am-6.30pm Monday to Friday and from 10am to around 2pm on Saturdays unless otherwise stated. Most shops are closed on Sunday, although supermarkets and some tourist shops on Main Street open seven days a week.

SUPERMARKETS

Gibraltar is a haven for UK ex-pats who reside in nearby Spain and regularly visit the Rock to stock up on many British goods on offer. Ironically, due to lower food prices across the border, many Gibraltarians tend to do their weekly grocery shopping in Spain.

Morrisons Supermarket

Open seven days a week and always packed to the brim with shoppers. The only British supermarket on the Rock.

Open: Mon-Sat: 8am-10pm
Sun: 9pm-7pm

Morrisons Supermarket
Westside Road
Gibraltar

Tel:	*Main Store*	*+350 200 41114*
	Pharmacy	*+350 200 75765*
	Filling Station	*+350 200 40756*

Coviran's Supermarket

Coviran took over the Peralta's supermarket chain which has been a national institution for decades. They sell UK as well as Spanish branded goods from their two stores, one in the South district near the BP Petrol Station and the other on Waterport Road beside the Evacuation memorial.

Coviran
104/107 New Harbours
Gibraltar
Tel. +350 200 48513

Coviran
Waterport Road
Gibraltar

Ramsons Minimarket

Ramsons minimarket is open till late most evenings, seven days a week and even on bank holidays. Despite the small size of its Watergardens store, it stocks fresh fruit and vegetables and sells fresh cuts of meat from its delicatessen counter. For a quick and inexpensive lunch, grab a hot chicken roll made with freshly baked bread.

Ramsons	**Ramsons**
Watergardens	*Casemates Square*
Waterport Road	*Gibraltar*
Gibraltar	
Tel. +350 200 71550	*Tel. +350 200 75721*
ramsons@gibtelecom.net	

BOOK SHOPS/NEWSAGENTS

Gibraltar has a few independent book shops and newsagents that stock local as well as international newspapers and magazines.

The Sky Shop at the Air Terminal, Morrisons and several of the larger petrol stations also offer a selection of international daily newspapers and magazines.

Gibraltar Book Shop

The Gibraltar Book Shop is Gibraltar's oldest and most comprehensive book store offering a decent selection of fiction and non-fiction titles and probably the most complete section of books about Gibraltar.

300 Main Street
Gibraltar
Tel. +350 200 71894
Fax +350 200 75554

Sacarello's Newsagent

This small newsagent on Main Street specializes in local and foreign newspapers, comics and magazines but also stocks a reasonable selection of fiction books.

96 Main Street
Gibraltar
Tel/Fax +350 200 78723

Gibraltar Museum Bookshop

A good selection of Gibraltar-interest books that focus primarily on Gibraltar's heritage and natural history.

18/20 Bomb House Lane
Gibraltar
Tel. +350 200 74298
Fax +350 200 79158
enquiries@museum.gib.gi

Terry's Bookshop

Second-hand book shop on Irish Town.

96 Irish Town
Gibraltar
Tel. +350 200 73701

Imperial Newsagency

Newsagent close to the Governor's Residence on the Rock (the Convent). Offers a selection of local and UK newspapers as well as stationery, etc.

291 Main Street
Gibraltar
Tel/Fax +350 200 78823

WH Smith

The classic British retailer has opened up the first Gibraltar branch of its well known newsagents in the Departure Lounge of Gibraltar's new Air Terminal. Selling magazines, snacks and books, including many local-interest editions, it is a welcome addition to the state-of-the-art terminal building.

Air Terminal
Winston Churchill Avenue
tel no. +350 200 11630
whsgib@hotmail.co.uk

Skyshop

Located at the Airport Terminal, this shop offers a good selection of local as well as foreign newspapers and a good selection of books.

Air Terminal
Winston Churchill Avenue
Gibraltar
Tel. +350 200 42639

Midtown Bookstore

Excellent book store located close in the centre of town near the Cornwalls Centre. Good selection of travel guides and local interest books.

Midtown Bookstore
11 Bell Lane
Gibraltar
Tel/Fax +350 200 60881

LOCAL CRAFTS

Gibraltar Crystal

The Gibraltar Crystal Factory, located on Casemates Square offers a unique opportunity to witness master glass blowers crafting molten glass into bespoke works of art. There are items to suit all tastes and price ranges and all products are genuinely hand crafted and come with their own certificate of authenticity.

Gibraltar Crystal

Casemates Barracks, Grand Casemates Square
Tel. +350 200 50136
gibcrystal@gibtelecom.net
www.gibraltarcrystal.com

Gibraltar Fine Arts Gallery

Hours: Monday-Friday, 11am-2pm and 4-6pm; Saturday, 11am-2pm

The Fine Arts Gallery located in the Upper walk at Casemates Barracks is a commercial art gallery but also showcases works by many of Gibraltar's leading artists. Set across two large rooms, other than the permanent collection, there are also regular themed exhibitions and displays by local and foreign artists.

Gibraltar Fine Arts Gallery
Units 13B & 14B
Grand Casemates Square
Gibraltar
Tel. +350 200 52126

The Nature Shop

There are two branches of the Nature Shop, one in Casemates and the other in the Gibraltar Botanic Gardens. Most items sold in these shops celebrate nature in some way and are crafted in an environmentally friendly manner. All profits generated by the Nature Shop are used towards the maintenance of the Alameda Botanical Gardens. The branch at the Botanic Gardens also has a cafeteria and sells plants and gardening materials.

The Nature Shop
First Floor
Casemates Shopping Centre
Gibraltar

The Nature Shop
Gibraltar Botanic Gardens
Grand Parade
Gibraltar

Tel. +350 200 41708
Fax +350 200 74022
natureshop@gibraltargardens.gi
www.gibraltargardens.gi/NatureShop

ELECTRONICS

There are a variety of shops on Gibraltar's Main Street offering electronic and hi-fi equipment, home cinema systems, personal computers, white goods and more. Below is just a small selection of them.

Khubchands
55/57 Main Street
Gibraltar
Tel. +350 200 78382

Oscar International
10 Casemates Square
Gibraltar
Tel. +350 200 72385

Sonic Electronic Limited
34 Main Street
Gibraltar
Tel. +350 200 73289

Bang & Olufsen
152 Main Street
Gibraltar
Tel. +350 200 78181

OTHERS

Pashmina

Located opposite the Gibraltar Court building at the far end of Main Street (near the Gibraltar Book Shop) this shop sells an interesting range of imported soft furnishings and decorations.

Pashmina
296 Main Street
Gibraltar
Tel. +350 200 40492

Out of Africa

On the first floor of the ICC building, this small unit sells various Moroccan and other North African goods. Perfect for those who do not get the chance to travel across to Morocco but wish to stock up on genuine African artefacts at reasonable prices.

Out of Africa
First Floor
International Commercial Centre
2A Main Street
Gibraltar
Tel/fax +350 200 47022

Princess Silks

Another Gibraltarian institution, Princess Silks, the drapery, curtain and up-holstery store on Main Street has been around for decades offering a huge selection of dressmaking fabrics at relatively low prices.

Princess Silks
212 Main Street
Gibraltar
Tel. +350 200 75041
Fax +350 200 70600

Chandra Gifts

Located in the upper town area, this little gem of a shop is worth seeking out for its selection of eastern imported good. Ranging from clothing and acces-sories to bracelets, stone pendants and earrings, you can be sure that the specially selected items will bring an Eastern flavour to your life. All items are sourced ethically from suppliers in Asia, mainly from India, Nepal or Tibet.

Chandra Gifts
64 Governor's Street
Gibraltar
tel no. +350 200 66111
email: chandragifts@hotmail.com

Tours

Dolphin Tours

Visitors to the Rock should not miss the opportunity to take a boat trip into the Bay and Strait to visit Gibraltar's thriving population of wild dolphins. Such is the abundance of dolphins that it is rare for boat trips to return to shore without having seen any of the three main species of dolphins found in the Bay. In fact it is not uncommon to see whole families of these friendly and inquisitive creatures, which will often approach and bow-ride in the waves created by boats. The boat tours themselves are worth their fee as they offer the chance to enjoy unique views of the Rock and its coastline from the sea. There are three main operators offering boat tours of the Bay of Gibraltar, with some also offering whale-watching tours. Dolphin tours are roughly 1.5 hours in duration whilst whale watching trips last around 3 hours. Most tours guides give a commentary with information about the dolphins and other wildlife. Larger groups may also be able to charter the dolphin boats for private tours.

For a fascinating account of a study of the dolphins in the Bay, the book 'One Man and His Boat' comes highly recommended. This account by local author Paul Linares covers a six year study of dolphins in the Bay of Gibraltar and includes with fabulous photographs together with many interesting anecdotes and memorable moments and findings.

Dolphin Adventure
Marina Bay
Gibraltar
Tel. +350 200 50650
E-mail info@dolphin.gi
www.dolphin.gi
Prices: £20 (adults), £10 (children under 12 years)

Dolphin Safari
Marina Bay
Gibraltar
Tel. +350 200 71914
Mobile +34 6072 90400

E-mail dolphin@gibraltar.gi
www.dolphinsafari.gi
Prices: £25 (adults), £12 ((children under 12 years - under 1: free)

Lower St Michael's Cave

Lower St Michael's Cave was discovered during World War II when a second entrance to the main cave was being blasted as part of preparations for its use as an emergency hospital. Unlike the upper chambers of St Michael's Cave, Lower St Michael's Cave can only be visited as part of a private tour. The tour, which costs just £5 per person, lasts about 3 hours and involves some crawling and minor climbing. Although the lower caves are fully lit, much of it remains in its original state with most known cave formations on show alongside a stunning underground lake. The tour is highly recommended for anyone wishing to see the interior of the Rock although it is certainly not for the faint of heart, as moving between the many interconnected chambers requires rope climbing, often with very few footholds. The trained guide will naturally assist if you have problems, but expect the occasional grazed knee or elbow.

The underground lake at the end of the tour is a spectacular sight but its edge can be very narrow (only about 15cm at some points) and it is not uncommon for visitors to fall into it, often to the amusement of other tour members. While the danger element is minimal, the tour is not recommended for the elderly or disabled, and children under the age of 10 years will generally not be admitted. Tours of Lower St Michael's Cave are available weekdays after 6pm and Saturdays from 2.30pm. These must be booked several days in advance by phoning one of the trained guides on the telephone numbers listed below. Tours cater to groups ranging from 5-10 persons although smaller groups can also sometimes be accommodated. You are advised to wear comfortable shoes (no sandals or high heels) and casual clothing.Photography is permitted.

Lower St. Michael's Cave
St Michael's Cave
Upper Rock Nature Reserve
Gibraltar
Tel. +350 200 56639000
*   +350 200 54231000*
*   +350 200 54004160*
Price: £5 per person.

The World War II Tunnels

During World War II Gibraltar was an important British naval and military base making the most of its position as gatekeeper of the Mediterranean Sea. During this period, mile upon mile of tunnels were blasted through the Rock giving military access to previously unreachable areas deep in the bowels of the Rock. You cannot help but follow in the footsteps of Winston Churchill and Charles De Gaulle and wonder at this feat of modern engineering, which comprises over 30mi of tunnels; a city within a city. Tours of approximately 2 hours in duration are conducted by a military guide at the price of £3 per person. Groups of between 6-15 people can be catered for although smaller groups can sometimes be accommodated. Tours must be arranged a couple of days in advance and this can be done by phoning one of the telephone numbers listed below. Visitors are advised to wear a comfortable pair of shoes and to bring a torch if possible.

The World War II Tunnels
Upper Rock Nature Reserve
Tel. +350 200 55820
Mobile +350 200 54011358
Fax +350 200 55828
Price: £3 per person.

Rock and Fortress Tunnel Tours

This tour is a slightly more commercial alternative to the World War II Tunnels and does not require advance booking. The tour includes exhibitions and photographic displays as well as entry to some areas of the Upper Rock that cannot be otherwise accessed. Tours run from Monday to Saturday and on regular occasions throughout the day between the hours of 10am-6pm. Visitors are accompanied by a licensed tour guide who will be able to answer any questions you may have about the tunnels or Gibraltar's military background. The tour lasts about an hour and includes a 15-minute break for refreshments.

Rock and Fortress Tunnel Tours
Hay's Level
Upper Rock Nature Reserve
Tel. +350 200 45957

Price: £8 for an hour long guided tour (but only available to those who have already paid the entrance fee to the Upper Rock)

Cable Car Tour

The quickest way to get to the summit, the cable car allows visitors to see the Upper Rock in its entirety with the flexibility of minimal time constraints. The cable car's top station is an ideal starting point for exploring the beauty of the Upper Rock, starting with the macaques' feeding area near the top station. St Michael's Cave, the Siege Tunnels and all the other Upper Rock attractions are a short walk away and visitors can then follow the walking path to town or hop back on the cable car at the summit or at the middle station near the Ape's Den. The journey itself to the cable car's top station, 400m above sea level, takes just 6 minutes. Once there you will be able to enjoy spectacular panoramic views from the top station's observation area across the Strait of Gibraltar to Africa. Visitors will also be able to take advantage of an interactive multimedia guide, which gives a guided commentary to the views from the top station's terraces. Multilingual commentary is available in eight languages including English, Spanish, French, Italian and German. There is also a small gift shop within the top station complex as well as a self-service restaurant. Group bookings can be taken in advance but tickets are best purchased on the day of travel from the cable car bottom station on Grand Parade. The cable car runs continuously to the top of the Rock every day from 9.30am-5.15pm (and till 7.15pm, April 1–October 31)

The Cable Car
Cable Car Bottom Station
Grand Parade
Gibraltar
Tel. +350 200 77826
E-mail wellstead@mhbland.com
Prices: Cable car only: £9.75 (adult return), £8 (adult single). £4.50 (child return), £4 (child single). Cable Car and Upper Rock attractions: £19.50 (adult return), £18 (adult single). £11.25 (child return), £10.75 (child single).

The Official Rock Tour by Taxi

A Taxi Tour of Gibraltar allows you to discover Gibraltar with your own personal tour guide who knows about the Rock's wildlife as well as everything there is to know about the Rock, past and present. The Official Tour is available from licensed taxi drivers who are easily located in the various starting points around the Rock. Most licensed taxi drivers will allow visitors to tailor-make their own tour and this can be done by either negotiating additions to the official tour or by arranging an alternative themed tour according to a visitor's own particular tastes.

The official tour will give visitors a brief look at many of Gibraltar's sites including compulsory stops on the East Side of the Rock including Catalan Bay, Europa Point and the Lighthouse as well as various stops in the Upper Rock Nature Reserve, which form the bulk of the tour. Visitors can also choose to visit the Alameda Botanical Gardens, Parson's Lodge and the Gibraltar Museum

There are various starting points around the Rock, these include the Frontier, Casemates Square, John Mackintosh Square (the Piazza), Cathedral Square and outside the Trafalgar Cemetery, as well as the cruise terminal and the Waterport Coach Park.

Gibraltar Taxi Association

Feetham House
19 Waterport Wharf
P.O. Box 602
Gibraltar
www.gibtaxi.com
Tel. +350 200 70052
Fax +350 200 76986
Prices: Approximately £10-15 per person (based on a minimum of 4 people). This includes entry to most of the main attractions. Prices are negotiable depending on the length of the tour proposed and indeed any additions made.

Directory

Accessibility

Although a good number of shops, hotels and attractions offer access for disabled use, not all do. Gibraltar's Old Town area can be particularly difficult for disabled visitors to access and it is advisable to check at one of the various Tourist Information offices before visiting any attraction with a wheelchair. A list of public toilets denoting those most easily accessible to disabled visitors can be found under Public Toilets, below. Many attractions, particularly in the Upper Rock have been notoriously difficult to modify to improve access for disabled visitors. Free access to the Upper Rock is offered to disabled people, by way of small compensation for this problem.

Shopmobility

Based in the ICC, the Shopmobility Centre offers for hire manual wheelchairs or powered scooters to those members of the public with disabilities, to elderly persons with walking impairments and to people with temporary disabilities through accident or illness. Bookings can only be made one day in advance and a passport will be required as a deposit.

Prices: £2 per day

Hours: 9.00am-1pm Mon to Friday. Closed Afternoons and Weekends.
Shopmobility Centre
Unit G4B, International Commercial Centre
Casemates Square
Gibraltar
Tel: +350 200 79898
E-mail eharrison@gibtelecom.net

Disability Awareness and Information Group
Tel. Mr E Rowbottom, +350 200 78980
*   Ms Amber Turner, +350 200 72020*
The Gibraltar Local Disability Movement
www.gibraltardisability.com
Tel. Mr Gordon Nelson, +350 200 74548
E-mail: gibraltarldm@gmail.com

Airline Offices

British Airways Gibraltar
Gibraltar Air Terminal
Gibraltar
Tel. +350 200 79300
www.ba.com

Monarch Airlines
Gibraltar Air Terminal Office
Winston Churchill Avenue
Gibraltar
Tel. +350 200 47477
Fax +350 200 70154
www.flymonarch.com

EasyJet Airlines
Bookings can be made through their website www.easyjet.com.

MH Bland
Cloister Building
Market Lane
Tel. +350 200 79478
Fax +350 200 71608
E-mail *info@mhbland.com*

Banks and ATMs

The following UK high street banks have offices in Gibraltar:

Barclays Bank
84/90 Main Street
Gibraltar
Tel. +350 200 78565
E-mail gibraltar@barclays.com

Lloyds TSB
First Floor Royal Ocean Plaza
Ocean Village
PO Box 482
Tel. +350 200 50999
E-mail europe@lloydstsb.com

Nat West Bank
57 Line Wall Road
PO Box 707
Tel. +350 200 77737
Fax +350 200 74557

The Royal Bank of Scotland
1 Corral Road
PO Box 766
Tel. +350 200 73200
Fax +350 200 70152

Cash withdrawals can be made from these banks' ATM machines, with the exception of Barclays Bank whose ATM can only be used by holders of bank accounts with Barclays Bank UK or Barclays Bank Gibraltar. There are additional cash machines at the Morrisons supermarket, at the BP petrol station on Winston Churchill Avenue and at the start of Main Street near the Venture Inn.

Camping and Caravans

Although there are plenty of quality campsites and caravan parks in nearby Spain, there are none whatsoever in Gibraltar. In fact, illegal camping is cracked down upon by the police and there are even restrictions on the entry of trailers and caravans into Gibraltar. Vehicles like these will not be allowed to enter Gibraltar unless customs dispensation is obtained and they are destined for private land. In addition, heavy traffic roads in Gibraltar have a maximum weight allowance of 32 tonnes.

Car Hire

Hiring a car is not essential for visitors who will be staying on the Rock and not venturing further than the neighbouring town of La Línea. However, those who wish to venture deep into Andalusia would be best advised to do so by car. Car hire in Gibraltar is a cost effective way of getting around and can be easily arranged in advance of or upon your arrival. The usual age requirements apply and cars are available to those aged between 23 and 75 and who are in possession of a valid driving licence that has been held for a minimum of 2 years.

AIM Rent A Car S.L.

Gibraltar Border
La Línea de la Concepción
Spain
www.aimrentacar.com
Gibraltar +350 200 57974000
UK +44 20 8 987 2807
Spain +34 628 904 914
Fax +350 200 79668
E-mail info@aimspain.com

Avis Rent A Car

Bayside Garage
Bayside Road
Gibraltar
www.avis.gi
Tel. +350 200 75552
Fax +350 200 77867
E-mail avis@gibnet.gi

Budget Rent A Car

Peninsular Rentals Ltd
P.O. Box 327
Gibraltar Airport
Gibraltar
www.budgetgibraltar.com
Tel. +350 200 79666
Fax +350 200 79668
E-mail budget@gibraltar.gi

GibCar.com
Gibraltar Airport
www.gibcar.com
E-mail bookings@gibcar.com

Prescott Limited Niza Car
Gibraltar Airport
Tel. +350 57537000
Fax +350 200 77926

Consolates and Embassies

Below is a list of the countries with consulates or honorary consulates in Gibraltar. Where no consulate exists, contact the relevant country's high commission or consulate in London.

Australia
Australian High Commission
Australia House, Strand
London WC2B 4LA
Tel. +44 20 7379 4334
Fax +44 20 7240 5333

Belgium
Honorary Consulate
47 Irish Town
PO Box 185
Gibraltar
Tel. +350 200 78353
Fax +350 200 77838

Canada
Canadian High Commission
1 Grosvenor Square
London W1K 4AB
Tel. +44 20 7258 6600

Denmark

Consulate
Cloister Building
Market Lane
PO Box 554
Gibraltar
Tel. +350 200 79478
Fax +350 200 71608

France
Consulate
209 Main Street
PO Box 135
Gibraltar
Tel. +350 200 78830
Fax +350 200 75867

Italy
Honorary Consulate
3 Irish Place
PO Box 437
Gibraltar
Tel. +350 200 47096
Fax +350 200 45591
E-mail *italy@gibraltar.gi*

Ireland
Irish Embassy
17 Grosvenor Place
London SW1X 7HR
Tel. +44 20 7235 2171

Norway
Honorary Consulate
Suite C, Ground Floor
Regal House
3 Queensway
Gibraltar
Tel. +350 200 48352
Fax +350 200 48347

E-mail *pls@millfield.gi*

Poland
Consulate
35 Governors Parade
Gibraltar
Tel. +350 200 74593
Fax +350 200 79491

South Africa
South African High Commission
South Africa House
Trafalgar Square
London WC2N 5DP
Tel. +44 20 7451 7299

Sweden
Consulate
Cloister building
Irish town
PO Box 212
Gibraltar
Tel. +350 200 72663
Fax +350 200 76189
E-mail *jpg@gibnet.gi*

Cultural Institutions

Amid much controversy locally, the Gibraltar Government announced the opening in Gibraltar of a branch of the Cervantes Institute, a non-profit organization aimed at the study and teaching of Spanish language and culture. The Institute, based in the Cloister Building on Irish Town (near the Victorian police Station), opened its doors in April 2011.

Customs Information

Visitors to the Rock will often stock up on duty-free goods. However, you should be aware that there are limits on the official amount of goods that Spanish and UK customs will allow you to import.

The following allowances are calculated on a per person basis

Importation from Gibraltar into Spain:
In addition to the alcohol and tobacco allowances listed below, you are allowed to import €171 worth of a variety of goods including perfume. Children under 17 years may import half this allowance but cannot have the tobacco or alcohol allowance. Officially, goods bought above the customs allowance in Gibraltar may only be imported into Spain between 9am-9pm.

Tobacco Products
200 cigarettes, or 50 cigars, or 250g of tobacco.

Alcoholic Beverages
1 litre of spirits or liqueurs over 22% volume, or 2 litres wine

Importation from Gibraltar into the UK
Whilst HM Customs Gibraltar will not check whether you are within your allowance at the airport in Gibraltar, there is a limit to the amount of goods that HM Customs & Excise in the UK will allow to be brought in from Gibraltar. Articles of any description of a value above £145 should also strictly be declared at customs in the UK.

Tobacco Products
200 cigarettes, or 100 cigarillos, or 50 cigars, or 250g of tobacco.

Alcoholic Beverages
2 litres of still table wine, or 1 litre of spirits or liqueurs over 22% volume, or 2 litres of fortified or sparkling wine or other liqueurs.

Perfume
60cc of perfume or 250cc of toilet water.

For further information or advice, contact

HM Customs Gibraltar
Customs House
Waterport
Gibraltar
Tel. +350 200 78879

Dentists

Dental treatment is not available free of charge on the Rock, but an emergency service is available at the Primary Care Centre for which only a nominal fee is charged. Below is a small selection of the privately run dental surgeries on the Rock. Be sure to book an appointment to avoid long waiting times.

Primary Care Centre
2nd Floor
International Commercial Centre
Casemates
Gibraltar
Tel. +350 200 70143 (ext. 3209)

Earle Dental Clinic
Second Floor
252/4 Main Street
Gibraltar
Tel. +350 200 79518
After hours: +350 200 79848

Mike Clark BDS
15D1 Baudelaire House
Town Range
Gibraltar
www.mikeclarkdental.com
Tel/Fax +350 200 52882

The Dental Care Centre
Suite 2
Princess House
216 Main Street
Gibraltar
Tel. +350 200 78844
Fax +350 200 70324
E-mail *dentalcare@gibtelecom.net*

The Dental Clinic

Neptune House
Marina Bay
Gibraltar
Tel. +350 200 76817
Fax +350 200 43799

Doctors/Medical Care/Hospital

European Union citizens visiting the Rock who are suddenly taken ill or have an accident during their time in Gibraltar have the right to see a doctor or receive general hospital treatment at St. Bernard's Hospital on the same terms as local people. In addition, free treatment is also available under Gibraltar Group Practice Medical Scheme at the Primary Care centre located in the ICC. A small charge is levied for the purchase of each medicinal item prescribed under this scheme. No specific vaccinations are required in order to gain entry to Gibraltar.

Primary Care Centre
2nd Floor
International Commercial Centre
Casemates
Tel. +350 200 72355 and +350 200 79700

St Bernard's Hospital
Harbour Views Road
Gibraltar
Tel. +350 200 79700

In addition there are a variety of private practices offering various medical services on the Rock:

GENERAL

College Clinic
Regal house
Queensway
Gibraltar
Tel. +350 200 77777
Fax +350 200 72791

E-mail *info@collegeclinic.gi*

Central Clinic Ltd
1A Centre Plaza
Horse Barrack Lane
Gibraltar
Tel. +350 200 59955
Fax +350 200 49495
E-mail *beguelin@gibtelecom.net*

Fit 4 Life Medical Centre
25 City Mill Lane
Gibraltar
Tel. +350 200 40463
Fax +350 200 75377

CHIROPRACTOR

Chiropractic Health Clinic
International Commercial Centre
2A Main Street
Gibraltar
www.gibraltarbackdoctor.com
Tel. +350 200 44226

PLASTIC SURGERY

Clinica Campos
C/o Valmar Pharmacy
11 Main Street
Gibraltar
Tel. +350 200 44471

SPORTS INJURY

Sports Injury Clinic
3/1 Governor's Parade
Gibraltar
Tel. +350 200 74555
E-mail *keithrehab@hotmail.com*

Electricity

Gibraltar uses UK three pin plugs as standard. Electricity in Gibraltar is 230 volts, alternating at 50 cycles per second. If you travel to Gibraltar with an electronic device that does not accept 230V at 50 Hertz a voltage converter will be needed.

Emergency Numbers

Fire and Ambulance: 190
Police: 199 or 112

Internet/Email

Café Cyberworld was Gibraltar's first commercial internet café on the Rock. Air-conditioned, it offers networked games and a fully licensed bar. It is conveniently located just a stone's throw from Casemates and is open 7 days a week from noon to midnight. Prices: 0.10p per minute.

Café Cyberworld
Units 14/16, Ocean Heights Gallery Arcade
Queensway
Gibraltar
Tel. +350 200 51416

The Call Shop, located at the southern end of Main Street near the Governor's Residence (the Convent), offers the only alternative commercial internet facilities for visitors to the Rock although many of Gibraltar's hotels also offer internet facilities

Call Shop Gibraltar
293A Main Street
Gibraltar
Tel. +350 200 49645

Library

Gibraltar's library is located in the John Mackintosh Hall at the southern end of Main Street. There is a reading area where you can read local and foreign daily newspapers free of charge. In order to withdraw books from the library, you will need to become a member, which can be applied for free of charge to residents of Gibraltar.

John Mackintosh Library
First Floor, John Mackintosh Hall
308 Main Street
Tel: +350 200 78000

Media (Newspapers/Radio/Television)

Gibraltar has two daily newspapers, the Gibraltar Chronicle and the Panorama. The Chronicle is Gibraltar's oldest established daily newspaper and the world's second oldest English Language newspaper to have been in continuous print; second only to The Times (UK). It was first published in 1801 and was famously the first to report news of Admiral Nelson's victory in the Battle of Trafalgar. The first edition of the Panorama was published in 1975.

In addition to the daily newspapers, there are other weekly newspapers such as the Vox and publications with strong political inclinations such as 7 days and the New People, which are both affiliated with local political parties. There are also a number of free monthly glossy magazines such as Gibraltar Magazine, Insight and Globe as well as various local business magazines such as B2B and Gibraltar International Magazine. Gibraltar has its own television station as well as a local radio station. GBC (television) begins broadcasting at 7.30pm with a number of locally-made shows including a news programme shown daily at 8.30pm. Radio Gibraltar is on the air 24 hours a day playing music on FM and MW frequencies as well as online via *www.gbc.gi*.

Radio Gibraltar Frequencies
91.3 FM   The Upper Rock and the City Centre
92.6 FM   The East Side and the Costa del Sol
100.5 FM South District and the Bay

Petrol Stations

There are a variety of petrol stations on the Rock, most of them outside the original city walls. Petrol is far cheaper in Gibraltar than in Spain and as a result hundreds of Spaniards cross the border into Gibraltar each day to fill their tanks, adding to the border queues and traffic congestion on Gibraltar's roads.

Pharmacies

Pharmacies are generally open Monday to Friday 9am-7pm, with one duty pharmacy opening each day until 9pm and during weekends. See the local media for information on the duty pharmacy. It should be noted that prescription drugs will not be sold without the appropriate paperwork and you should see a GP locally at the health centre or the Gibraltar Hospital.

Baglietto Pharmacy
61 Governor's Street
Gibraltar
Tel. +350 200 76822

Bell Pharmacy
27 Bell Lane
Gibraltar
Tel. +350 200 77289
Fax +350 200 42989

Calpe Pharmacy Limited
93 Main Street
Gibraltar
Tel. +350 200 77230
Fax +350 200 41376

232 Main Street
Gibraltar
Tel. +350 200 77231
Fax +350 200 47231

Unit G9
International Commercial Centre, Gibraltar
Tel/Fax +350 200 77977

Crown Pharmacy

4 Casemates Square
Gibraltar
Tel. +350 200 78598
Fax +350 200 42512
Louis' Pharmacy
Unit F12, International Commercial Centre
Tel. +350 200 44797
Fax +350 200 44845

Mill Pharmacy
21/21a City Mill Lane
Gibraltar
Tel/Fax +350 200 50554

New Chemist
19 Main Street
Gibraltar
Tel. +350 200 45039

Trafalgar Pharmacy
48/50 Main Street
Gibraltar
Tel. +350 200 71710
Fax +350 200 71714

Valmar Pharmacy
11A Main Street
Tel. +350 200 74971
Fax +350 200 70370

Police

There are two police stations, one on Irish Town near John Mackintosh Square
(the Piazza) and one at New Mole House, which is on Rosia Road near the
100-ton gun. In addition, there are police on the beat in the Main Street area
24 hours a day and on Casemates Square on Friday and Saturday nights. For
police emergencies ring 199 or 112. If you park illegally and your car is towed
away, you should contact Gibraltar Security Services Limited.

Royal Gibraltar Police
Police Headquarters
New Mole House
Rosia Road
Gibraltar
Tel. +350 200 72500

Royal Gibraltar Police
Central Police Station, Irish Town
Gibraltar
Tel. +350 200 79394

Gibraltar Security Services Limited
Queensway Car Park, Reclamation Road
Tel. +350 200 76999
After Hours +350 588 57000

Post Offices

Gibraltar's main post office is situated on Main Street between Tuckey's Lane and Bell Lane. In addition to traditional post office services, there is also retail outlet for the Gibraltar Philatelic Bureau, which sells many commemorative Gibraltar coins, stamps and first-day covers. There are two further Post Offices in the North district within Glacis Estate and the South district on Scud Hill.

Royal Gibraltar Post Office
104 Main Street
Tel. +350 200 75714

North District Post Office
Glacis Estate
Tel. +200 350 71385

South District Post Office
Scud Hill
Gibraltar
Tel. +200 350 73974

Gibraltar Philatelic Bureau
Suite 9/11, Block 2, Watergardens
Waterport
Tel. +350 200 75662
Fax +350 200 42149

Public Toilets

Below is a list of Public Toilets in Gibraltar. Those marked with an asterisk denote public toilets accessible to disabled people.

Alameda Gardens
Air Gibraltar Terminal*
Camp Bay
Casemates Square*
Catalan Bay (during the bathing season only)*
Eastern Beach (during the bathing season only)*
International Commercial Centre*
John Mackintosh Hall*
John Mackintosh Square (the Piazza)*
Kings Bastion Leisure Centre*
Line Wall Road (opposite Duke of Kent House)
Little Bay
Market Place*
St Michael's Cave*
Trafalgar Cemetery (opposite)

In addition there are several automated 'paid' public toilets located around the city in the area of the frontier, Winston Churchill Avenue, Waterport Road, Eurotowers, Commonwealth Parade car park and Grand Parade. The fee for the use of the toilet is 50p or 1 Euro.

Student Organizations

Gibraltar Students Association
Montagu Bastion
Tel. +350 200 76732
E-mail *gsa@gibtelecom.net*

Taxis

Gibraltar Taxi Association (24 Hour Service)
Tel. +350 200 70027 or +350 200 70077
Fax +350 200 76986

In addition, there are taxi ranks at the frontier, Casemates Square, John Mackintosh Square (Piazza), Cathedral Square and at Charles V Wall by the Trafalgar Cemetery.

Telephone

The country dialling code for Gibraltar is +350. The following useful numbers can be dialled from a local telephone:

Fire and Ambulance: 190
Police: 199 or 112

Local Directory Enquiries: 195
International Directory Enquiries: 196
Operator Assistance: 100
Talking Clock: 150

Time

Gibraltar's standard time zone is GMT+1 and it operates daylight saving time from spring to autumn.

Travel Agents

There are a variety of travel agents in Gibraltar that organize tours and can assist with flight bookings and other onward travel options.

Sterling Travel
18/20 John Mackintosh Square (the Piazza)
Tel. +350 200 71787
Fax +350 200 76445
E-mail *sterlinggib@sterling-travel.com*
www.sterling-travel.com

– Nearby Spain –

La Línea (de la Concepción)

La Línea, or La Línea de la Concepción to give it its full title, is the first stop as you cross the land frontier from Gibraltar into Spain. It is part of the province of Cadiz in Andalusia but was originally nothing more than a line of fortifications built to separate British Gibraltar from mainland Spain. In recent years it has flourished into a sizeable modern town that dwarfs its British neighbour in size, and has a population at around 65,000—more than double that of Gibraltar.

Soaring property prices on the Rock have driven many Gibraltarians to relocate to La Línea or within its suburbs in areas such as Santa Margarita and Alcaidesa. This has changed the make-up of the town, which now boasts a multicultural community of linenses (people from La Línea) living side by side with Gibraltarians as well as foreigners from further afield who work on the Rock but have chosen to make La Línea their home. A large number of Linenses journey across the border daily to work in Gibraltar where wages are traditionally higher than they are in Spain. As a result of this, La Línea has become a thriving community with a vibrant night life and a large number of high-end restaurants and tapas bars.

History

La Línea's history does not stem back much further than 1704 when Gibraltar was taken from the Spanish and a permanent garrison town began to be established in the area. The fortifications included the fortresses of Santa Barbara and San Felipe, which were completed by Philip V in 1735. The fortified defensive line that connected the two fortresses extended from east to west across the isthmus and the guns along this line prevented English ships from docking outside the port of Gibraltar. Thus La Línea de Contravalación ("fortification line") came into existence but it was not until 1913 that it was given its current name by King Alfonso XIII because the Immaculate Conception of Mary was the Spanish army's patron saint. Over the years it increased in size from a small insignificant hamlet to its current size.

You can still see the remnants of the Fort of Santa Barbara on the eastern side of La Línea by the municipal football stadium. The Fort was largely destroyed by the British together with the Fort of San Felipe during the Spanish War of Independence (1804-14) to prevent them falling into the hands of Napoleon's belligerent French army. A wooden walkway has been built over the remains of the Fort of Santa Barbara's, which intermingles with an

extensive bunker system that dates back to World War II and extends into the area of the **Parque Princesa Sofia** which is in front of you on your right hand side as you cross the frontier into Spain. There is also a further series of bunkers, gun positions and pillboxes in the Park, which were developed between 1940 and 1944 and lie derelict among the rusty remains of Spanish and French cannons.

Linenses have traditionally found work in Gibraltar and this was especially true when Gibraltar was an important naval port and manual labour was much in demand. The closure of the border by the Spanish government between 1969 and 1982 meant that most Spaniards who worked on the Rock lost their jobs overnight. This had a profoundly negative effect on the area, which became one of the poorest areas of Andalusia. Since the border was fully reopened in 1985 many Linenses have once again begun seeking employment in Gibraltar, injecting a significant cash boost into the area. With demand for housing spilling across from Gibraltar and many shops and restaurants catering to wealthier Gibraltarians, the cost of living has risen dramatically in La Línea in recent years.

Beaches

The town of La Línea has a long seafront comprising mainly the west coastline, which overlooks Algeciras and the Bay of Gibraltar, and an eastern coastline

with the Mediterranean Sea. For those who wish to avoid the hustle and bustle of the La Línea beaches, there are more secluded beaches to be found if you follow the eastern coast up towards Santa Margarita and Alcaidesa.

The west coast has undergone some regeneration in recent years with a new Paseo Maritimo (seaside walkway) and the addition of many new amenities for beach goers. Nevertheless, the Playa de Espigón just a few metres from the frontier queue loop is still considered by many to be a no-swim area due to suspected contamination levels in the water from the nearby oil refinery. Much has been done by the local authorities to rid the beach of pollution (as well as its bad reputation), but for many this remains very much in the memory.

It is the eastern coastline of La Línea, generally referred to as Playa de Levante, that attracts most of La Línea's beach goers. This beach, which essentially extends for miles up the eastern coast, begins at the area known as Playa de San Felipe, separated from Gibraltar's Eastern Beach by the airport's runway and the small area of no-man's land. The same beach continues, albeit with different names from Playa de Santa Barbara on which the ruins of the fort of the same name are still visible to Playa de La Atunara on the edge of **La Atunara** fishing village. The beach ends temporarily and there is a small port of fishing boats before a lengthy stretch of coastline extends all the way to Playa de la Alcaidesa. There is a watchtower built along this coastline near the residential area of Santa Margarita, which dates back to 1630.

Attractions

In Plaza Cruz Herrara in the centre of town, you can find the Museo del Istmo located in a former police headquarters. It has some interesting displays relating to the local area including a model of the Rock of Gibraltar built in the 1940s. There is also a large bullring in the centre of the town that attracts large crowds and a Museo Taurino ("museum of bullfighting") on Calle Mateo Inurria, which is open Tuesday to Saturday 11.30am-3pm. The parish **Church of the Inmaculada Concepción** (built in 1879) is on Calle Sol and the statue of the three ladies on the square that it fronts is a tribute to the artist Jose Cruz Herrera who was born in La Línea.

The Atunara area of La Línea, which developed around the town's fishing quarter, has preserved its fishing culture and a visit to the small harbour with its many brightly-coloured fishing boats is well worth the effort. However, the highlight of La Atunara is the many bars and restaurants that specialize in fresh seafood dishes. Seafood enthusiasts will be spoilt for choice with restaurants to suit everybody's tastes and pockets.

Shopping

La Línea has a compact shopping area, based around Calle Real and Plaza Cruz Herrara. There is a limited amount of Spanish high-street shops but it is mainly made up of smaller independent stores. The market place is, like in many Spanish towns, the central hub of activity from Monday to Saturday until around 2pm, with a large outdoor market (Miercoles Loco; "Mad Wednesday") to be found every Wednesday morning along Avenida Principe.

Eating

As well as the excellent fish restaurants in the La Atunara area, there are a number of quality restaurants and tapas bars that specialize in meat dishes in the La Línea area. La Chimenea on Calle Moreno de Mora is a particular favourite amongst the tapas bars as is the Argentinean-themed Patagonia on Calle Carboneros. As far as restaurants are concerned there can be few better than El Tendio a taxi ride away in Campamento or alternatively El Comedor de Enrique with their Menu Degustación ("tasting menu"), on Avenida Maria Guerrero.

San Roque

San Roque is the nearest of the so-called White Villages of Andalusia, so named because of their characteristic Andalusian whitewashed architecture and their charming narrow streets. It is very typical of the area and with plenty of local bars and restaurants is a perfect place to get a flavour of nearby Andalusia, right on Gibraltar's doorstep. Its bullring, built in 1853 is one of the oldest in Andalusia. In addition the Pinar del Rey ("The King's Pineforest") with its many varieties of indigenous flora and fauna offers outstanding bird-watching opportunities. This village can be reached by following the western coast out of La Línea on Avenida Principe de Asturias until you reach the E-15 and then follow the signs that lead into the centro ciudad.

History

The history of the municipality of San Roque, like that of so many of its close neighbours, dates back many centuries. The ruined town of Carteia nearby was an important settlement in prehistoric times going on to become an important Phoenician and later a Carthaginian trade post. The ruins of the once great city of Carteia, positioned just south of the town of San Roque near the CEPSA oil refinery, were only discovered in 1927 and the majority of it remains unexcavated.